SUPER EASY SONGBOOK

POP STANDARDS

ISBN 978-1-4950-9435-4

HAL•LEONARD®

7777 W. BLUEMOUND RD. P.O. BOX 13819 MILWAUKEE, WI 53213

Visit Hal Leonard Online at
www.halleonard.com

Welcome to the *Super Easy Songbook* series!

This unique collection will help you play your favorite songs quickly and easily. Here's how it works:

- Play the simplified melody with your right hand. Letter names appear inside each note to assist you.

- There are no key signatures to worry about! If a sharp ♯ or flat ♭ is needed, it is shown beside the note each time.

- There are no page turns, so your hands never have to leave the keyboard.

- If two notes are connected by a tie ⌣, hold the first note for the combined number of beats. (The second note does not show a letter name since it is not re-struck.)

- Add basic chords with your left hand using the provided keyboard diagrams. Chord voicings have been carefully chosen to minimize hand movement.

- The left-hand rhythm is up to you, and chord notes can be played together or separately. Be creative!

- If the chords sound muddy, move your left hand an octave* higher. If this gets in the way of playing the melody, move your right hand an octave higher as well.

  An octave spans eight notes. If your starting note is C, the next C to the right is an octave higher.

———————————————— ALSO AVAILABLE ————————————————

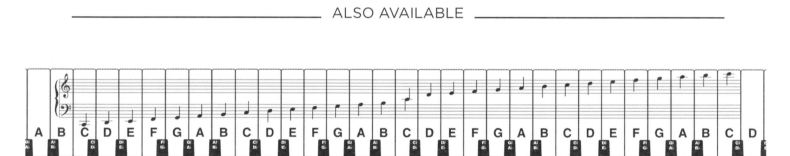

Hal Leonard Student Keyboard Guide HL00296039

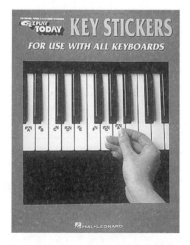

Key Stickers HL00100016

Africa

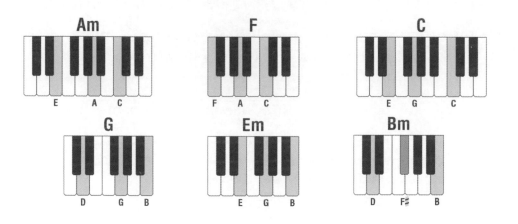

Words and Music by David Paich
and Jeff Porcaro

Moderately

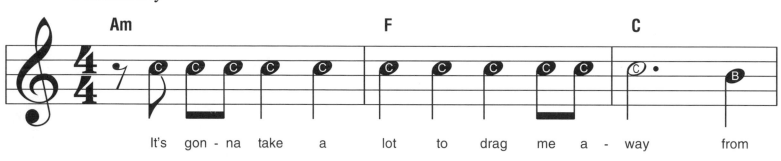

It's gon - na take a lot to drag me a - way from

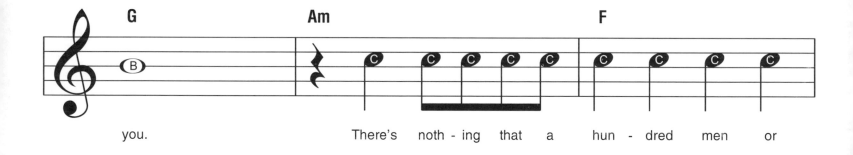

you. There's noth - ing that a hun - dred men or

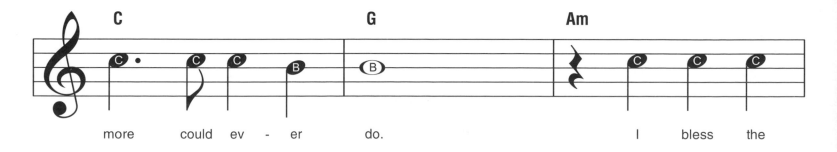

more could ev - er do. I bless the

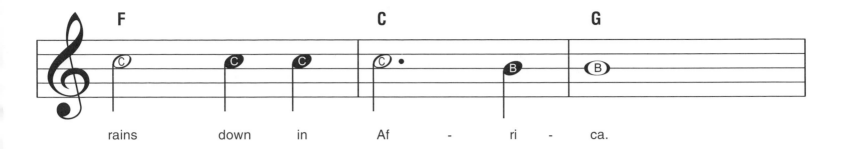

rains   down   in   Af - ri - ca.

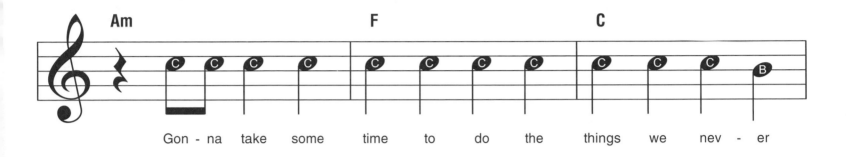

Gon - na take some   time to do the   things we nev - er

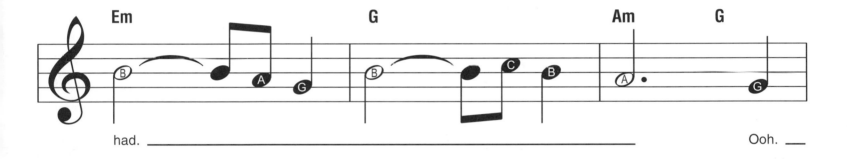

had. _____   Ooh. __

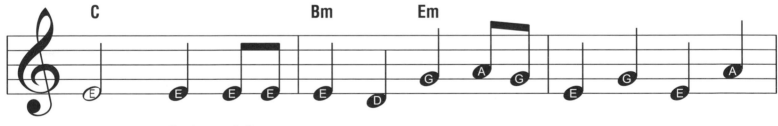

___   *(Instrumental)*

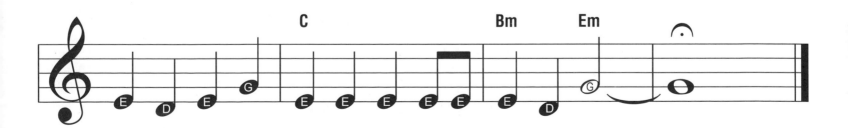

Ain't No Sunshine

Words and Music by
Bill Withers

Alone Again
(Naturally)

Words and Music by
Gilbert O'Sullivan

Moderate Pop beat

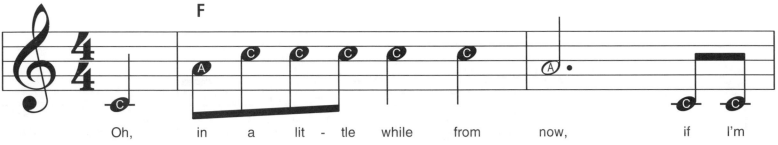

Oh, in a lit-tle while from now, if I'm

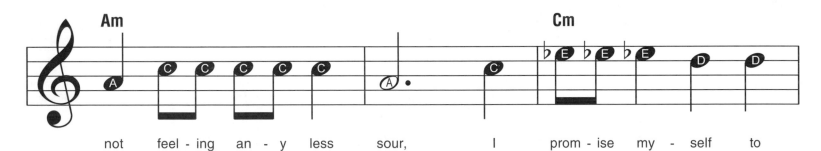

not feel-ing an-y less sour, I prom-ise my-self to

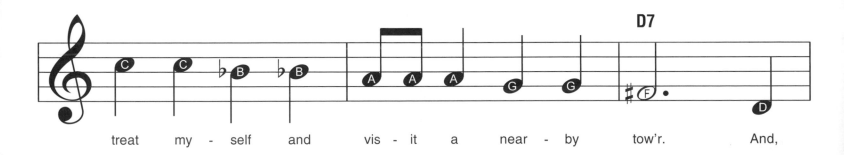

treat my-self and vis-it a near-by tow'r. And,

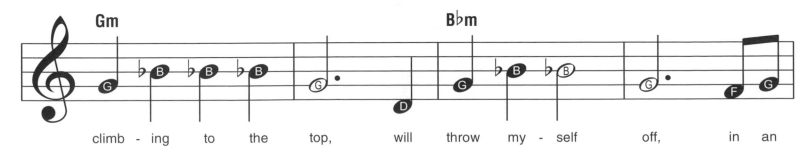

climb-ing to the top, will throw my-self off, in an

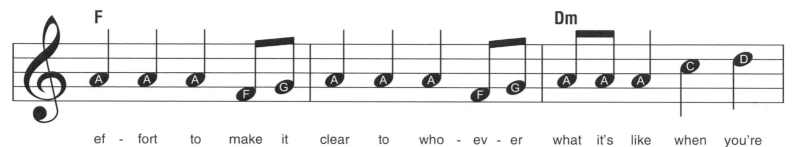

ef - fort to make it clear to who - ev - er what it's like when you're

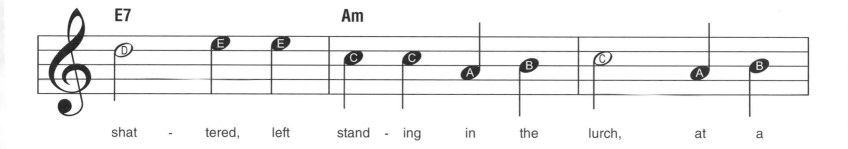

shat - tered, left stand - ing in the lurch, at a

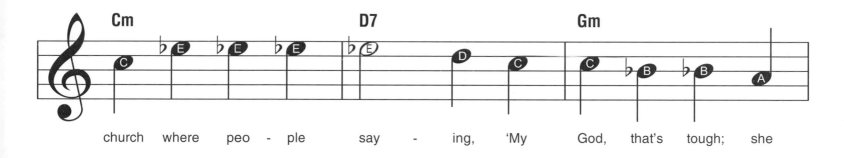

church where peo - ple say - ing, 'My God, that's tough; she

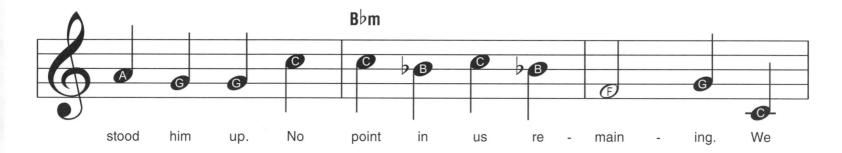

stood him up. No point in us re - main - ing. We

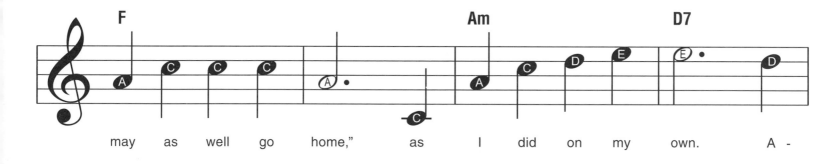

may as well go home," as I did on my own. A -

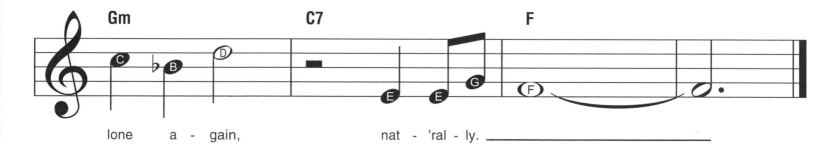

lone a - gain, nat - 'ral - ly. _____

Bridge Over Troubled Water

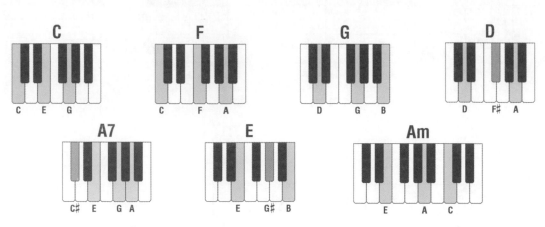

C   F   G   D

A7   E   Am

Words and Music by
Paul Simon

Moderately

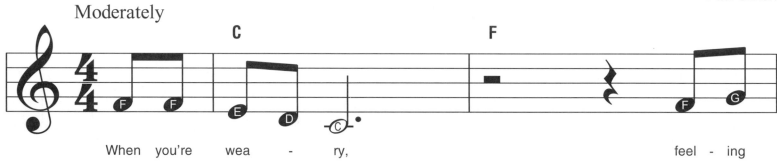

When you're wea - ry,   feel - ing

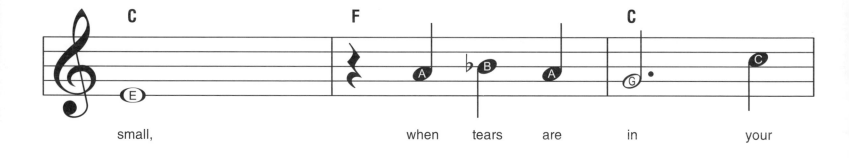

small,   when tears are in your

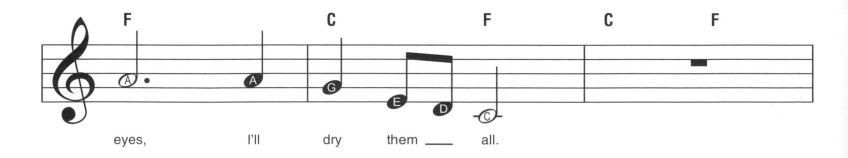

eyes, I'll dry them ___ all.

13

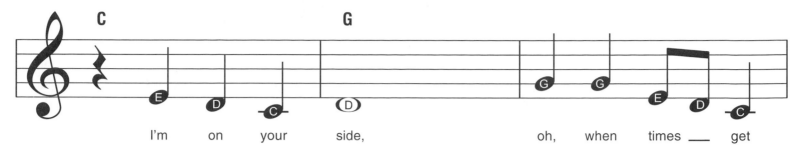

I'm on your side, oh, when times ___ get

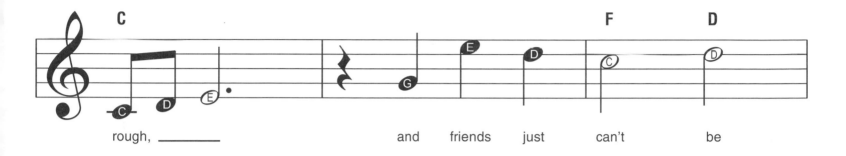

rough, _____ and friends just can't be

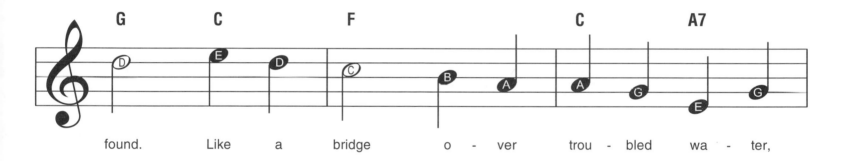

found. Like a bridge o - ver trou - bled wa - ter,

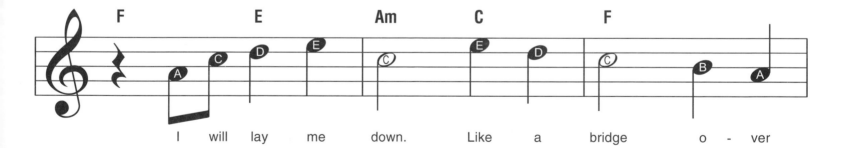

I will lay me down. Like a bridge o - ver

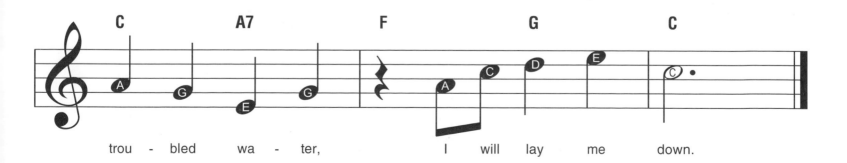

trou - bled wa - ter, I will lay me down.

Can't Help Falling in Love

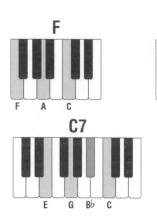
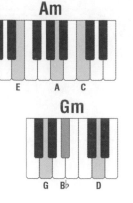
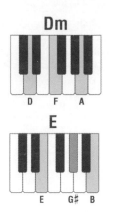
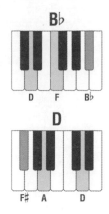

Words and Music by George David Weiss,
Hugo Peretti and Luigi Creatore

Moderately

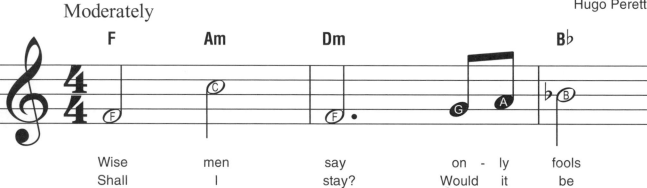

Wise men say on - ly fools rush
Shall I stay? Would it be a

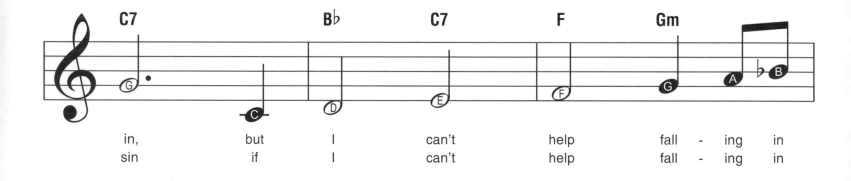

in, but I can't help fall - ing in
sin if I can't help fall - ing in

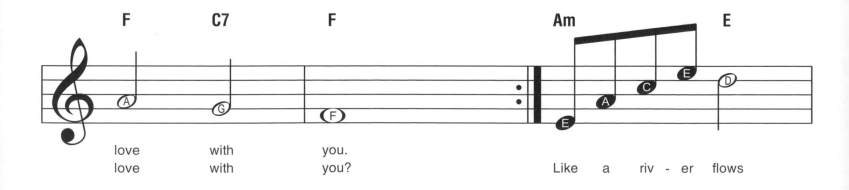

love with you.
love with you? Like a riv - er flows

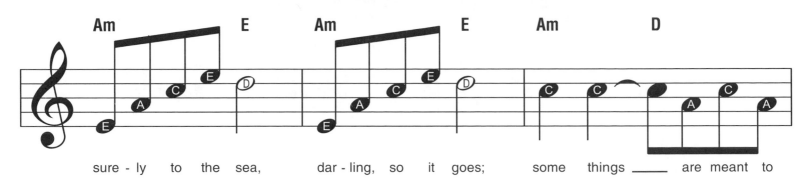

sure - ly   to   the   sea,   dar - ling,   so   it   goes;   some   things _____ are   meant   to

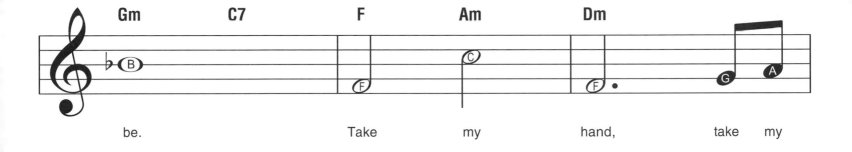

be.   Take   my   hand,   take   my

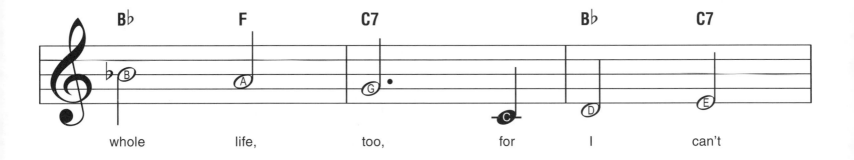

whole   life,   too,   for   I   can't

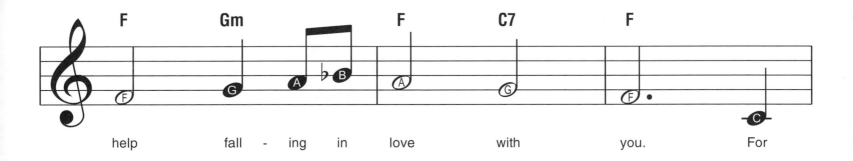

help   fall - ing   in   love   with   you.   For

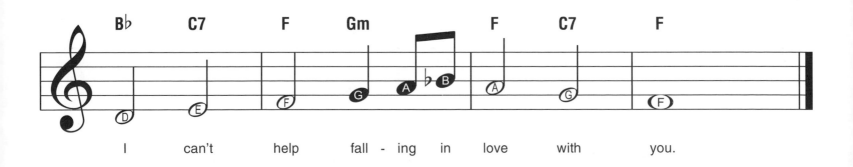

I   can't   help   fall - ing   in   love   with   you.

Candle in the Wind

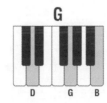 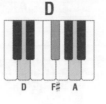 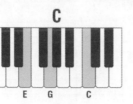 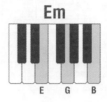

Words and Music by Elton John
and Bernie Taupin

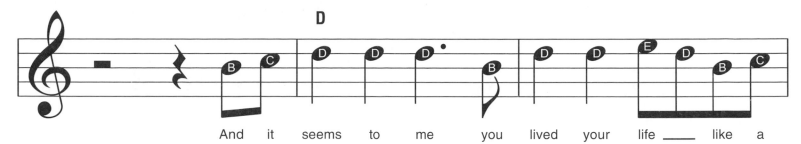

And it seems to me you lived your life ____ like a

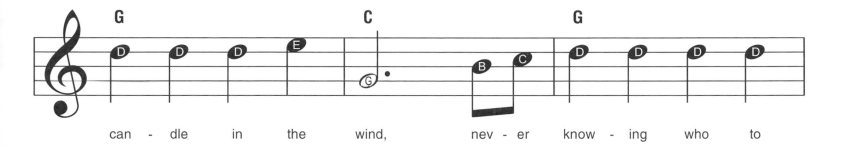

can - dle in the wind, nev - er know - ing who to

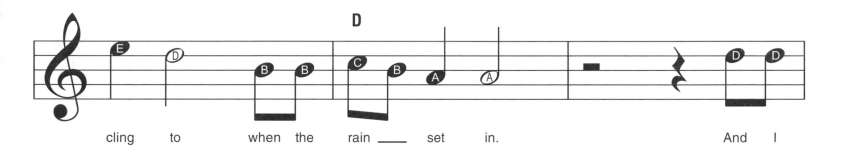

cling to when the rain ____ set in. And I

would have liked to've known you, but I was just ____ a kid. Your

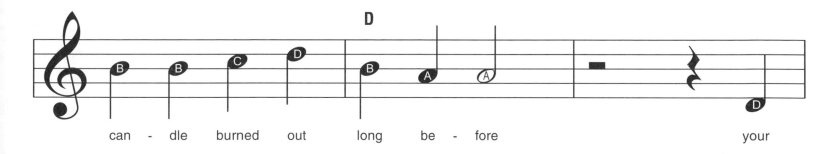

can - dle burned out long be - fore your

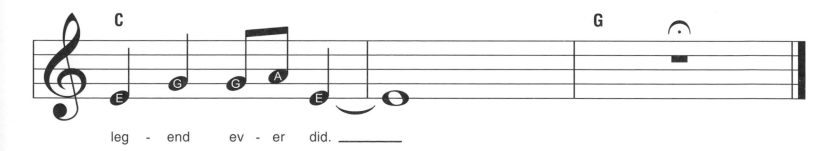

leg - end ev - er did. ____

Careless Whisper

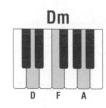
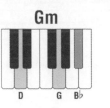
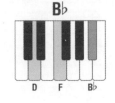
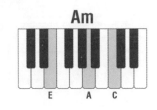

Words and Music by George Michael
and Andrew Ridgeley

Moderately

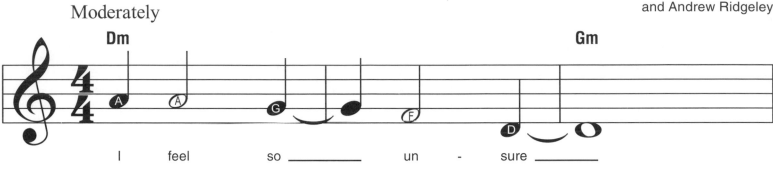

I feel so _____ un - sure _____

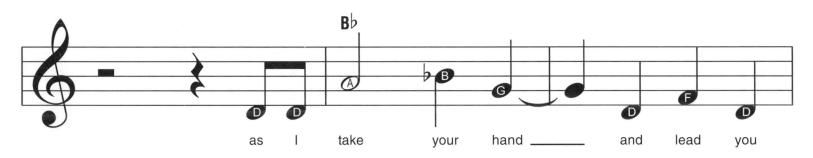

as I take your hand _____ and lead you

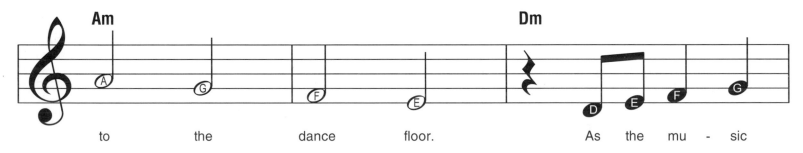

to the dance floor. As the mu - sic

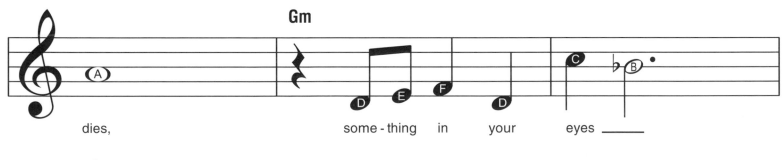

dies, some - thing in your eyes _____

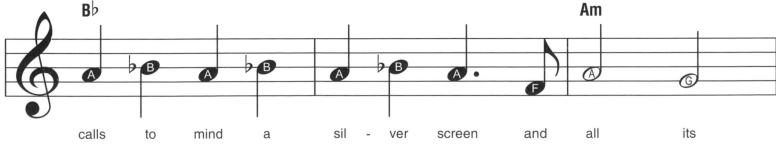

calls to mind a sil - ver screen and all its

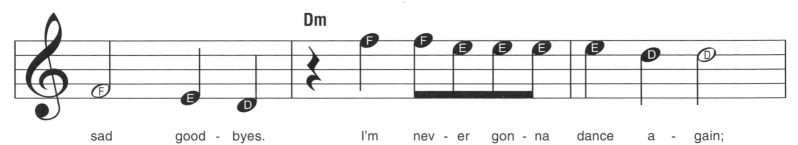

sad good - byes. I'm nev - er gon - na dance a - gain;

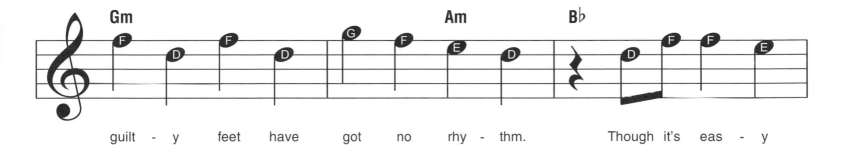

guilt - y feet have got no rhy - thm. Though it's eas - y

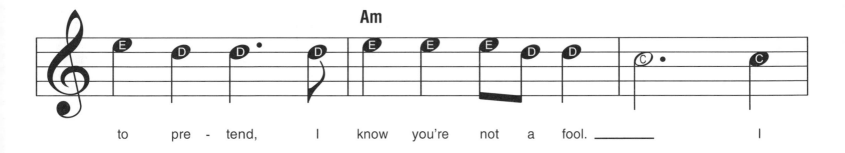

to pre - tend, I know you're not a fool. _____ I

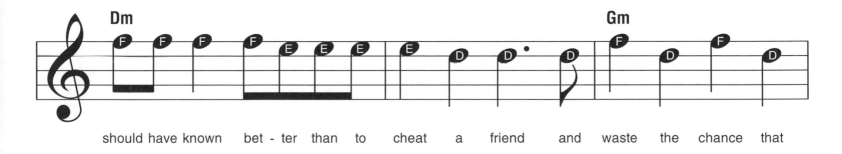

should have known bet - ter than to cheat a friend and waste the chance that

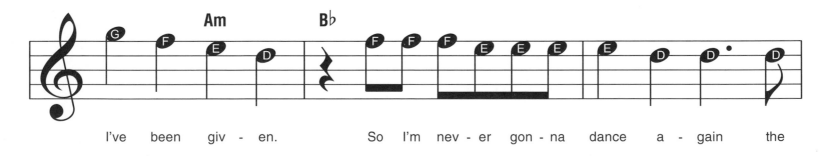

I've been giv - en. So I'm nev - er gon - na dance a - gain the

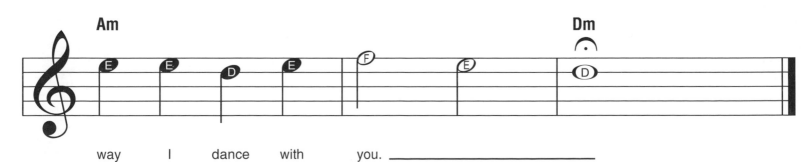

way I dance with you. _____

Copacabana
(At the Copa)

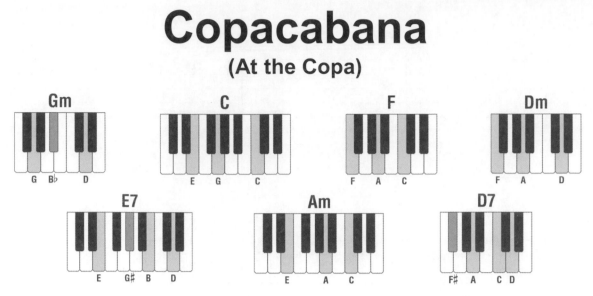

Music by Barry Manilow
Lyric by Bruce Sussman and Jack Feldman

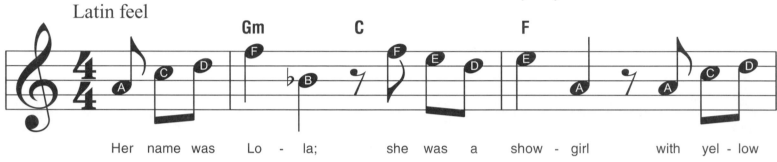

Her name was Lo - la; she was a show - girl with yel - low

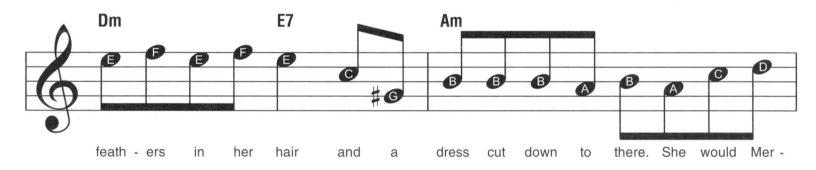

feath - ers in her hair and a dress cut down to there. She would Mer -

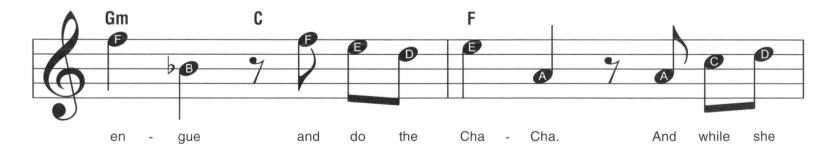

en - gue and do the Cha - Cha. And while she

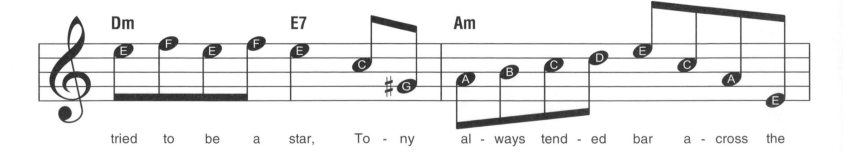

tried to be a star, To - ny al - ways tend - ed bar a - cross the

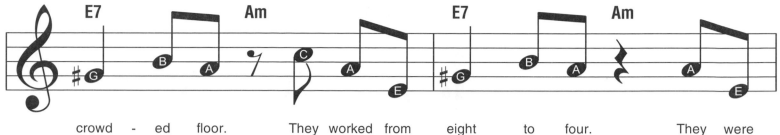

crowd - ed floor. They worked from eight to four. They were

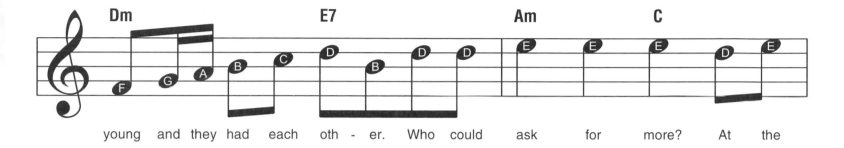

young and they had each oth - er. Who could ask for more? At the

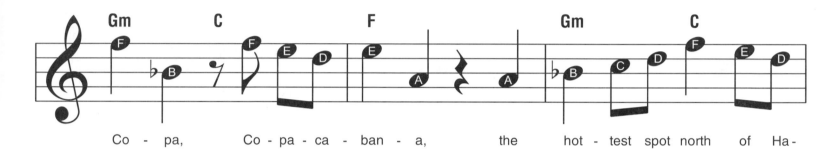

Co - pa, Co - pa - ca - ban - a, the hot - test spot north of Ha-

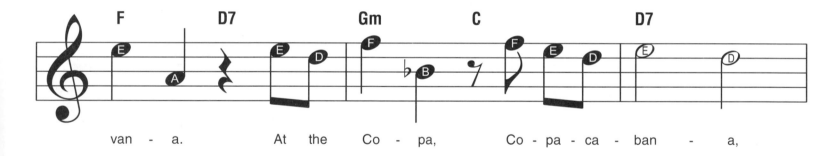

van - a. At the Co - pa, Co - pa - ca - ban - a,

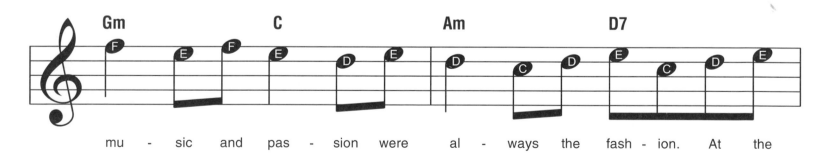

mu - sic and pas - sion were al - ways the fash - ion. At the

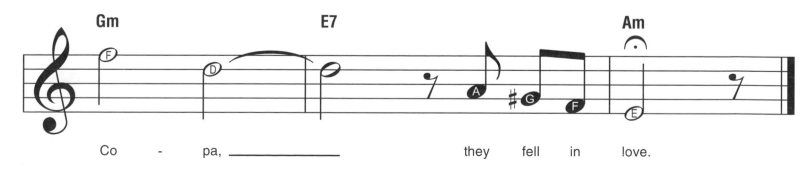

Co - pa, _____ they fell in love.

Crazy

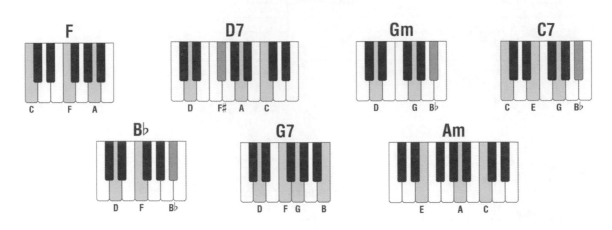

Words and Music by
Willie Nelson

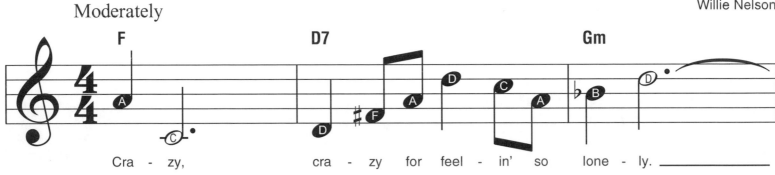

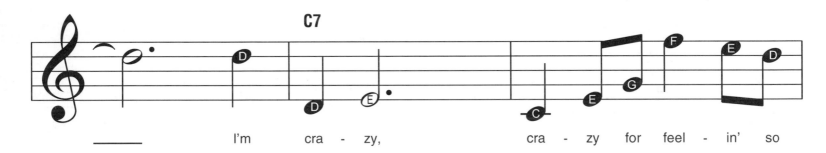

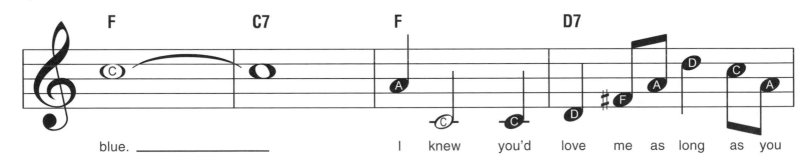

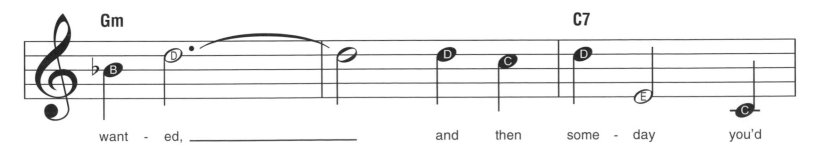

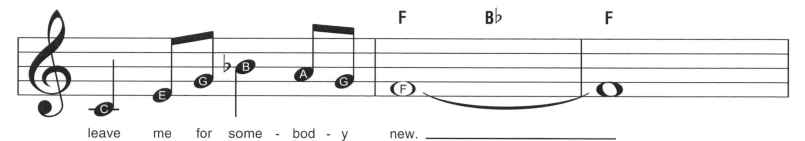

leave me for some - bod - y new. _____

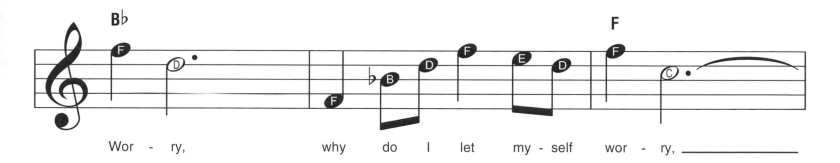

Wor - ry, why do I let my - self wor - ry, _____

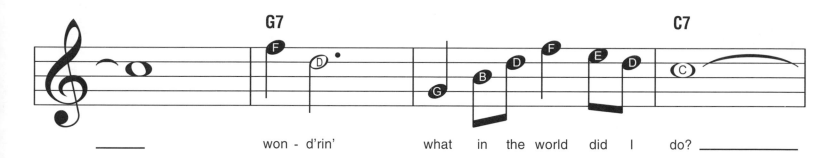

_____ won - d'rin' what in the world did I do? _____

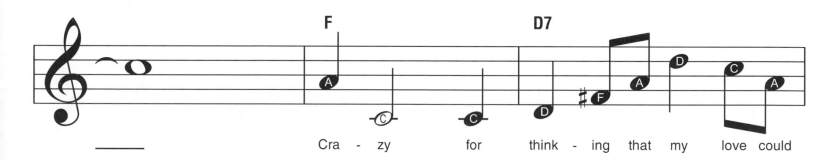

_____ Cra - zy for think - ing that my love could

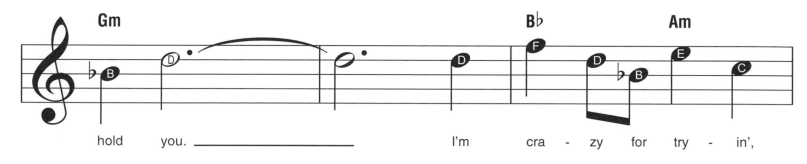

hold you. _____ I'm cra - zy for try - in',

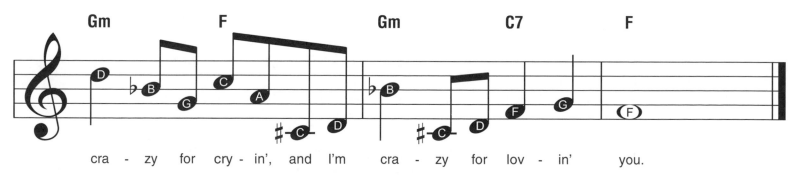

cra - zy for cry - in', and I'm cra - zy for lov - in' you.

Crazy Little Thing Called Love

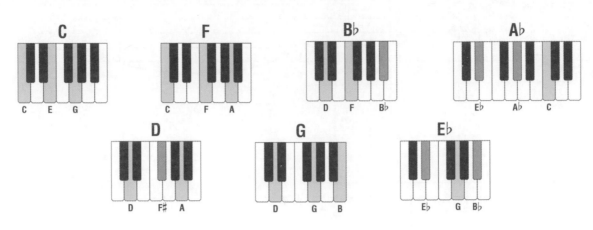

Words and Music by
Freddie Mercury

Moderately fast Shuffle

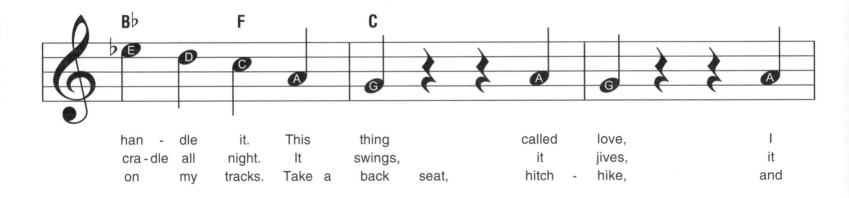

This thing called love, I just can't
thing called love, it just cries in a
cool, re-lax, get hip, get

han-dle it. This thing called love, I
cra-dle all night. It thing swings, it jives, it
on my tracks. Take a back seat, hitch-hike, and

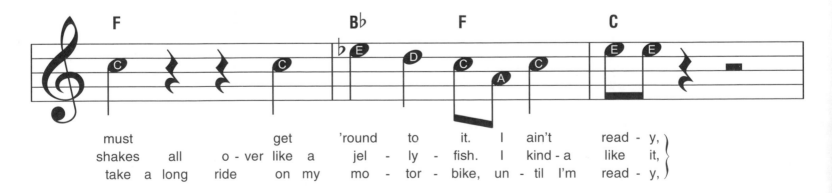

must get 'round to it. I ain't read-y,
shakes all o-ver like a jel-ly-fish. I kind-a like it,
take a long ride on my mo-tor-bike, un-til I'm read-y,

Don't Dream It's Over

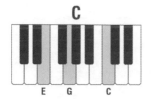
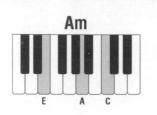
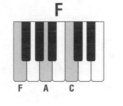
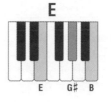
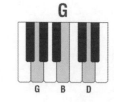

Words and Music by
Neil Finn

Moderately

There is free-dom with-in, _____ there is

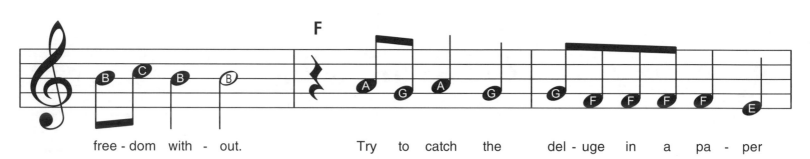

free-dom with-out. Try to catch the del-uge in a pa-per

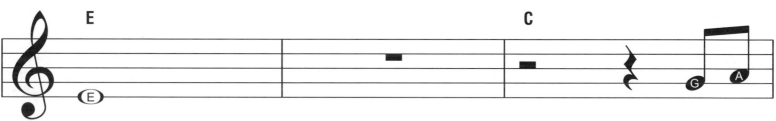

cup. There's a

bat-tle a - head. _____ Man - y bat-tles are lost,

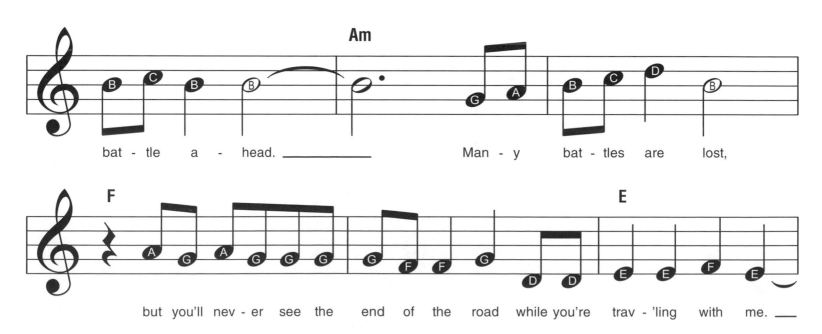

but you'll nev - er see the end of the road while you're trav-'ling with me. ___

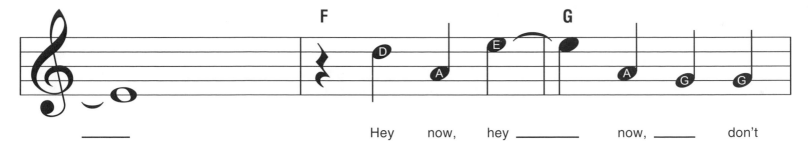

_____ Hey now, hey _____ now, _____ don't

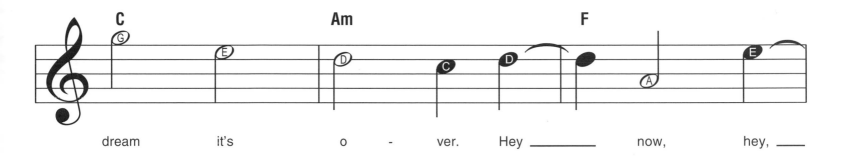

dream it's o - ver. Hey _____ now, hey, _____

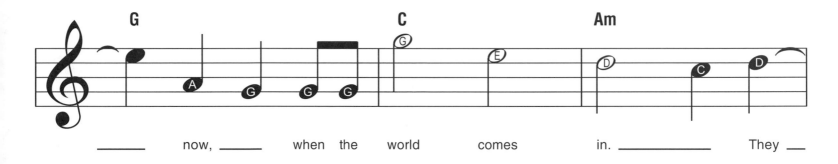

_____ now, _____ when the world comes in. _____ They __

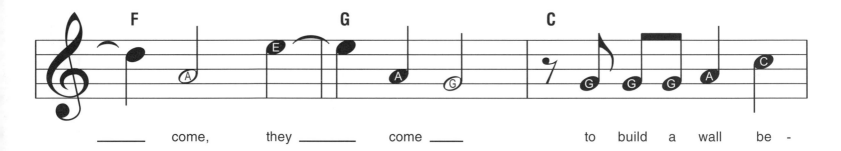

_____ come, they _____ come _____ to build a wall be -

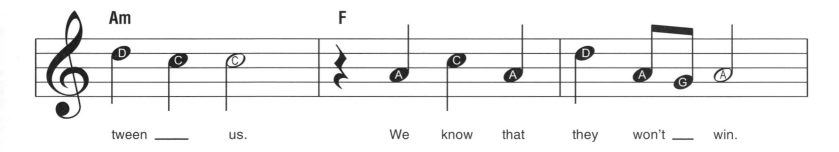

tween _____ us. We know that they won't _ win.

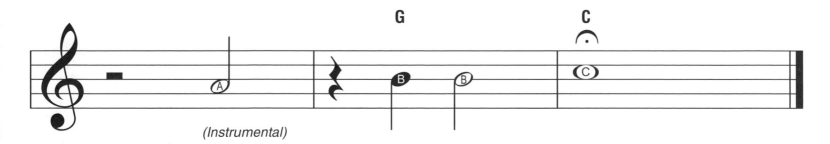

(Instrumental)

Don't Know Why

Words and Music by
Jesse Harris

Dream a Little Dream of Me

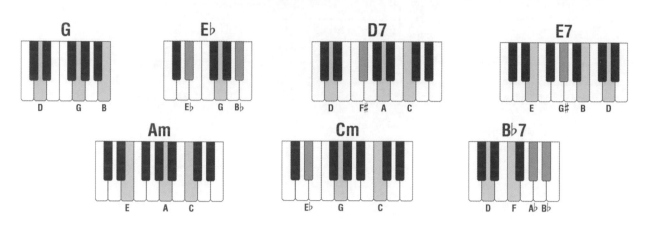

Words by Gus Kahn
Music by Wilbur Schwandt and Fabian Andree

Moderate Shuffle

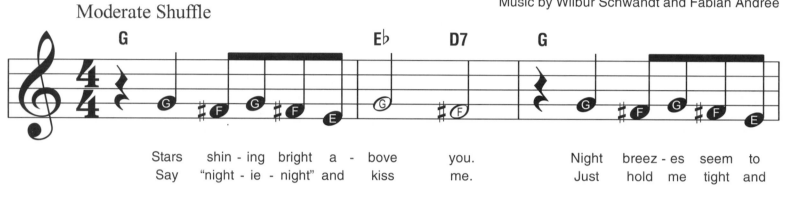

Stars shin-ing bright a-bove you. Night breez-es seem to
Say "night-ie-night" and kiss me. Just hold me tight and

whis-per, "I love you." Birds sing-ing in the syc-a-more tree.
tell me you'll miss me. While I'm a-lone and blue as can be,

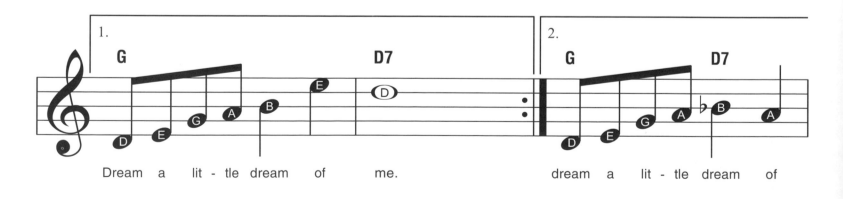

1.
Dream a lit-tle dream of me.

2.
dream a lit-tle dream of

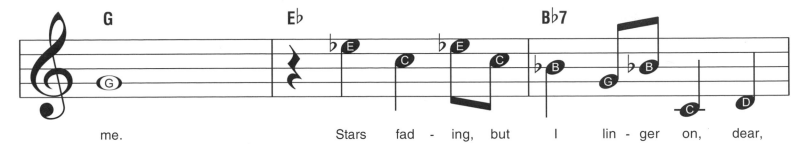

me.   Stars fad - ing, but   I   lin - ger on,   dear,

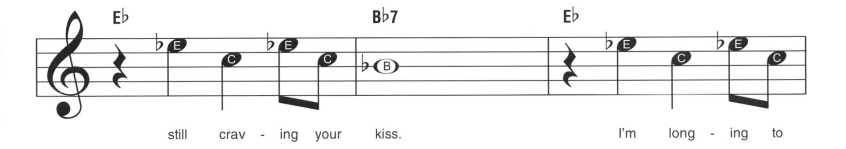

still   crav - ing your   kiss.   I'm   long - ing to

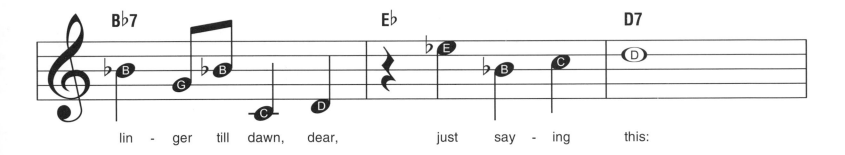

lin - ger till dawn, dear,   just say - ing   this:

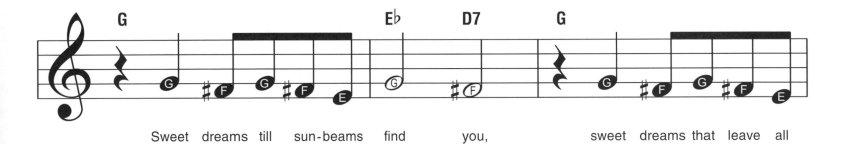

Sweet dreams till sun - beams find   you,   sweet dreams that leave all

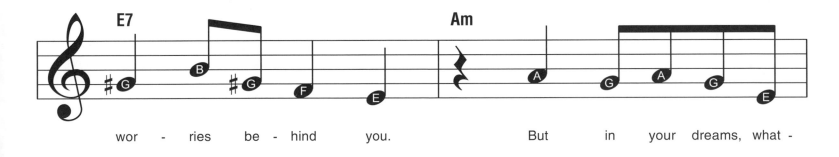

wor - ries be - hind you.   But   in   your dreams, what -

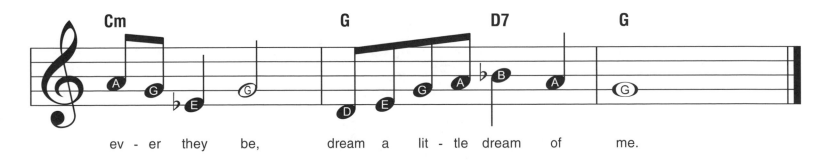

ev - er they be,   dream a lit - tle dream of   me.

Every Breath You Take

Music and Lyrics by
Sting

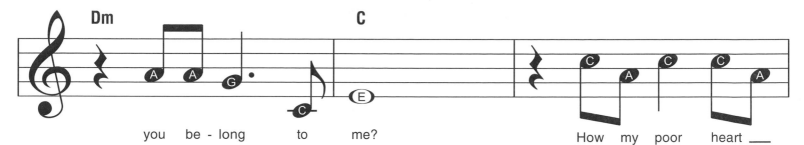

you be - long to me? How my poor heart ___

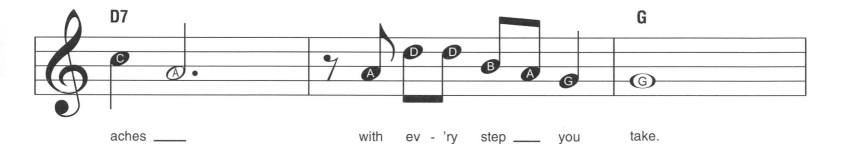

aches ___ with ev - 'ry step ___ you take.

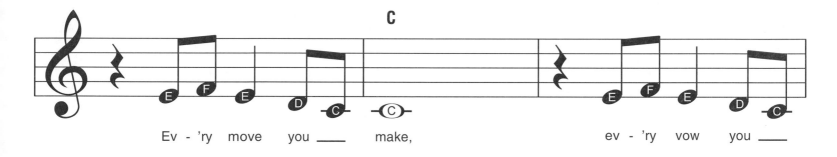

Ev - 'ry move you ___ make, ev - 'ry vow you ___

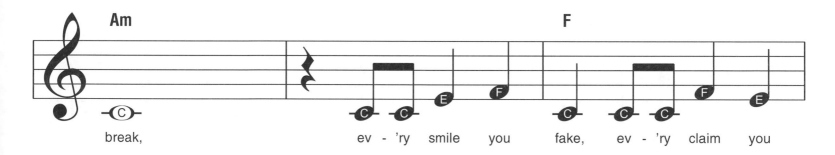

break, ev - 'ry smile you fake, ev - 'ry claim you

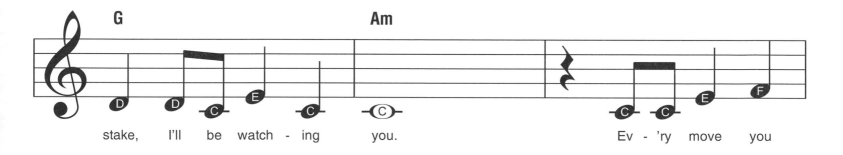

stake, I'll be watch - ing you. Ev - 'ry move you

make, ev - 'ry step you take, I'll be watch - ing you. ___

Fields of Gold

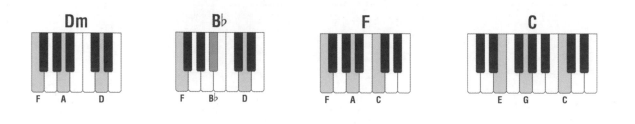

Music and Lyrics by
Sting

You'll re - mem - ber me when the west wind moves up -
took her me love when for to gaze a while up -

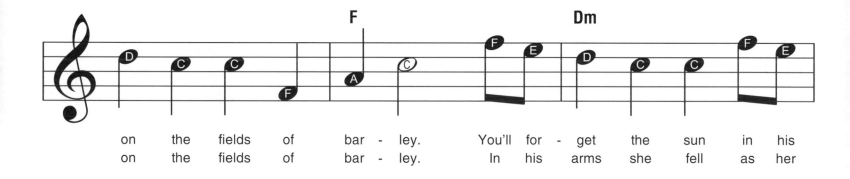

on the fields of bar - ley. You'll for - get the sun in his
on the fields of bar - ley. In his get arms she fell as her

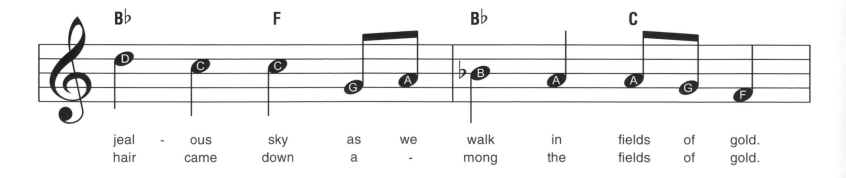

jeal - ous sky as we walk in fields of gold.
hair came down a - mong the fields of gold.

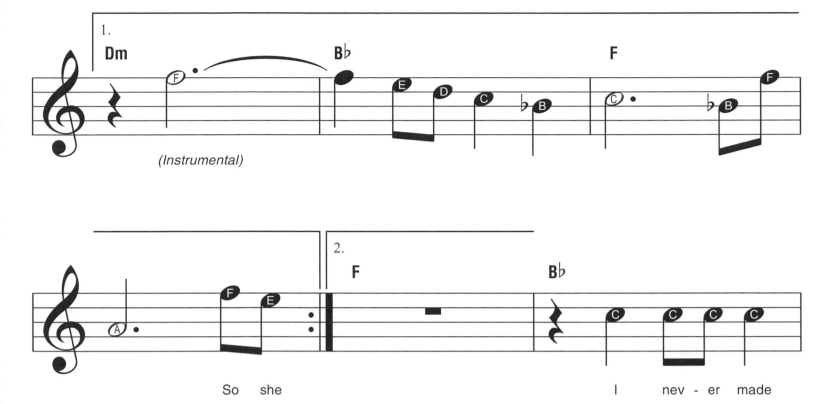

(Instrumental)

So she

I nev - er made

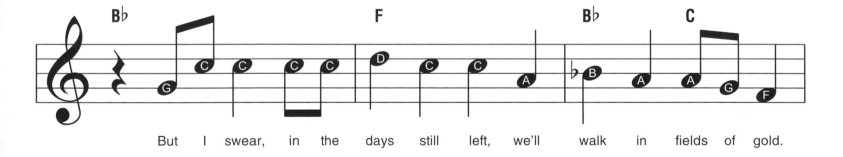

prom - is - es light - ly, and there have been some that I've bro - ken.

But I swear, in the days still left, we'll walk in fields of gold.

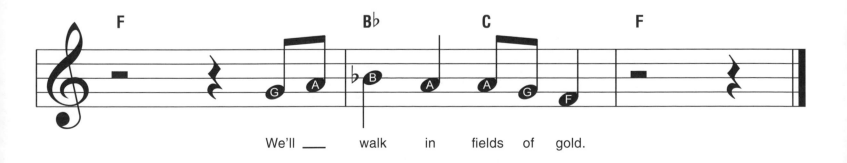

We'll ___ walk in fields of gold.

God Only Knows

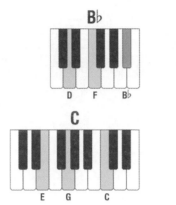
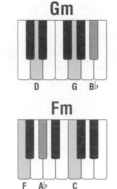
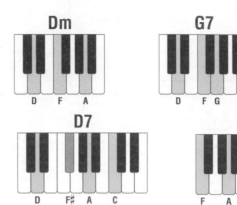
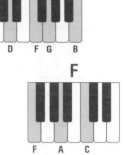

Words and Music by Brian Wilson
and Tony Asher

Moderately fast Shuffle

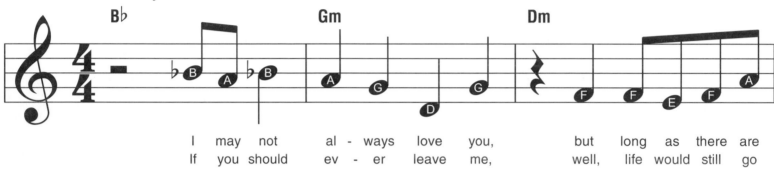

I may not al - ways love you, but long as there are
If you should ev - er leave me, well, life would still go

stars a - bove you, you'll nev - er need to doubt it.
on, be - lieve me. The world could show noth - ing to me,

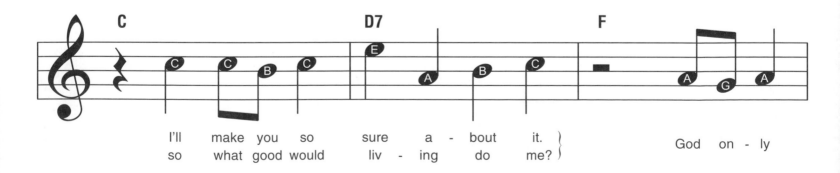

I'll make you so sure a - bout it.
so what good would liv - ing do me? } God on - ly

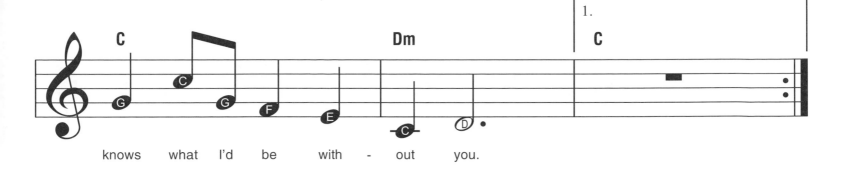

knows   what   I'd   be   with - out   you.

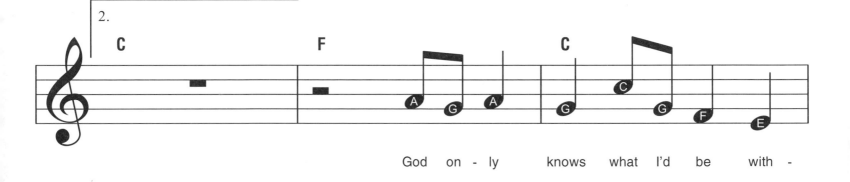

God   on - ly   knows   what   I'd   be   with -

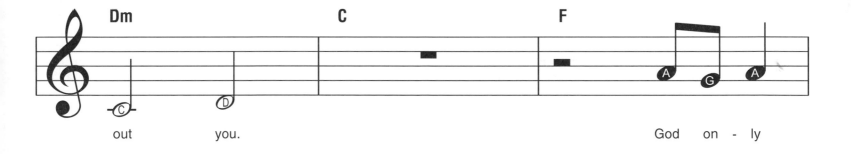

out   you.   God   on - ly

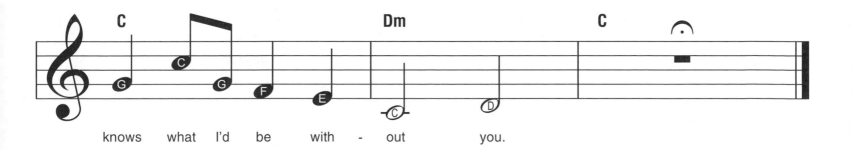

knows   what   I'd   be   with - out   you.

Hallelujah

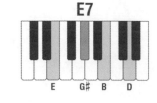

Words and Music by
Leonard Cohen

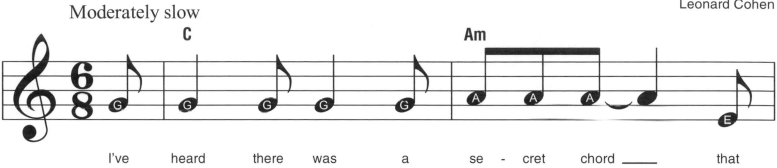

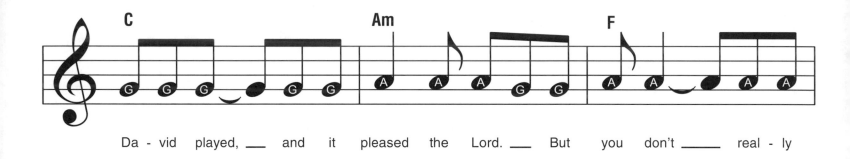

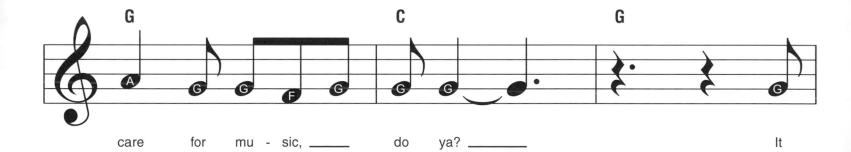

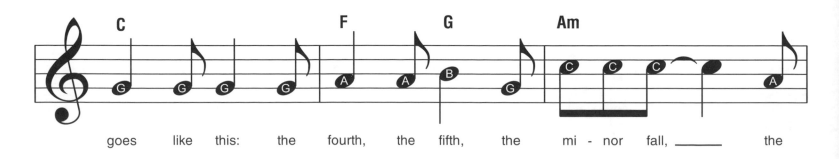

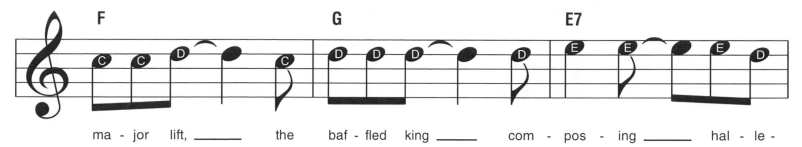

ma - jor lift, _____ the baf - fled king _____ com - pos - ing _____ hal - le -

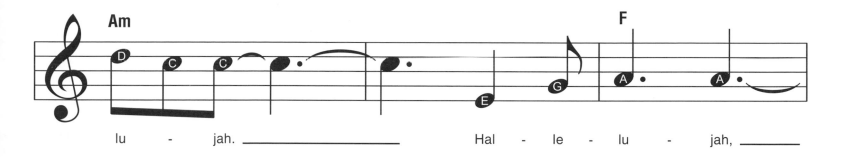

lu - jah. _____ Hal - le - lu - jah, _____

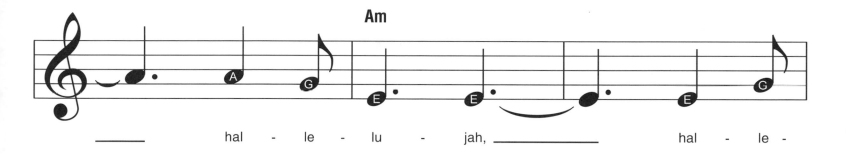

_____ hal - le - lu - jah, _____ hal - le -

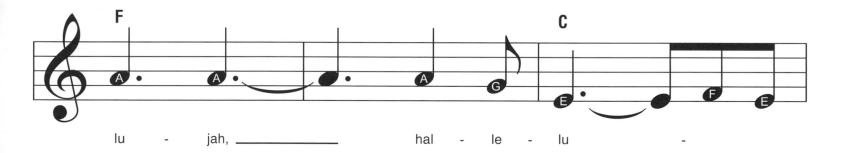

lu - jah, _____ hal - le - lu -

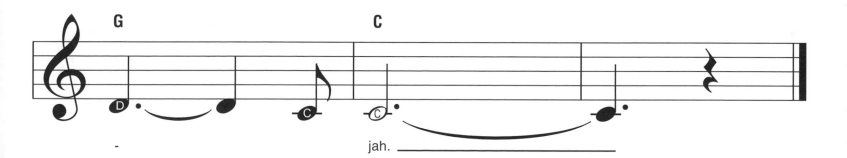

- jah. _____

Have I Told You Lately

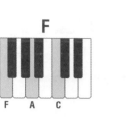
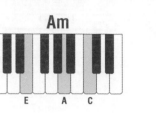
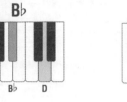
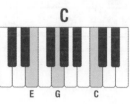
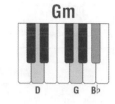

Words and Music by
Van Morrison

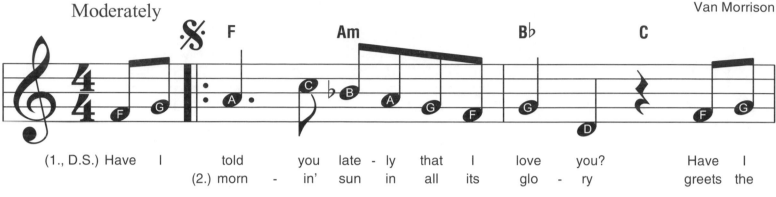

(1., D.S.) Have I told you late-ly that I love you? Have I
(2.) morn - in' sun in all its glo - ry greets the

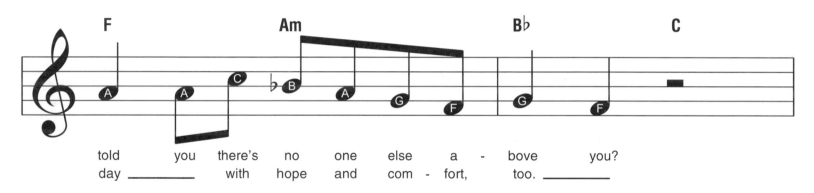

told you there's no one else a - bove you?
day _____ with hope and com - fort, too. _____

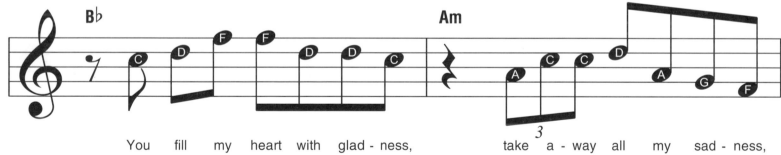

You fill my heart with glad - ness, take a - way all my sad - ness,
You fill my life with laugh - ter and some-how you make it bet - ter,

ease my trou - bles, that's what you do. For the
ease my trou - bles, that's what you

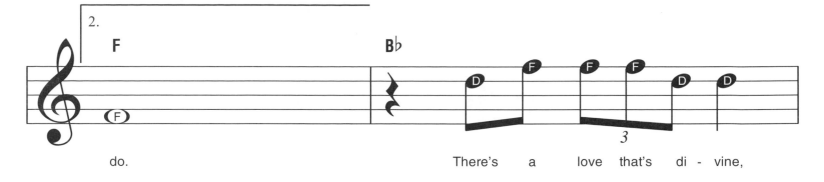

do.

There's a love that's di - vine,

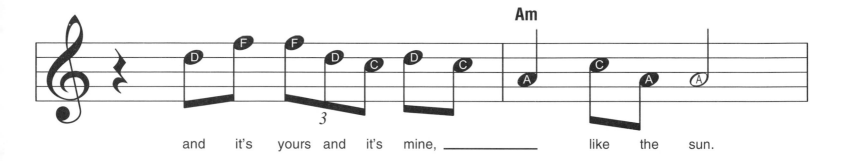

and it's yours and it's mine, ___ like the sun.

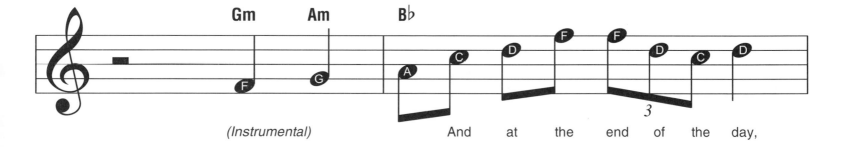

(Instrumental) And at the end of the day,

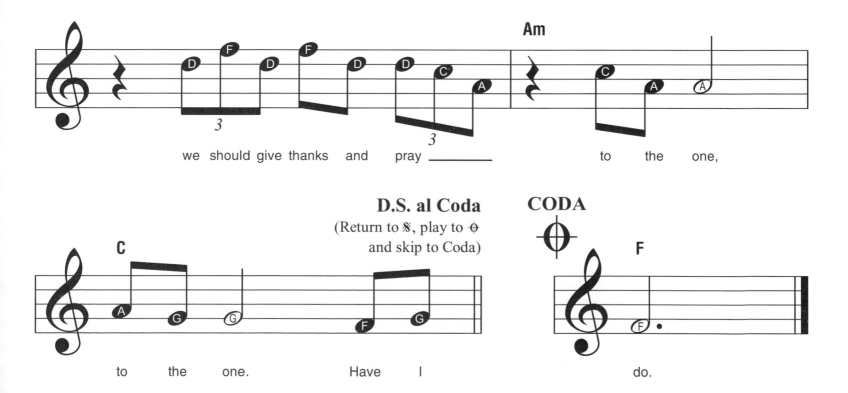

we should give thanks and pray ___ to the one,

D.S. al Coda
(Return to 𝄋, play to ⊕
and skip to Coda)

CODA

to the one. Have I

do.

Holding Back the Years

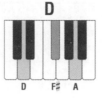

Words by Mick Hucknall
Music by Mick Hucknall and Neil Moss

Moderately

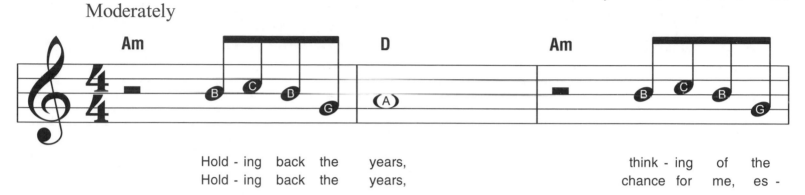

Hold - ing back the years,   think - ing of the
Hold - ing back the years,   chance for me, es -

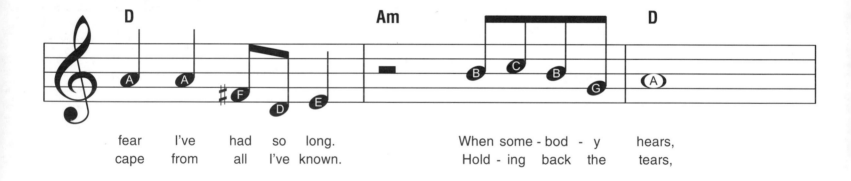

fear I've had so long.   When some - bod - y hears,
cape from all I've known.   Hold - ing back the tears,

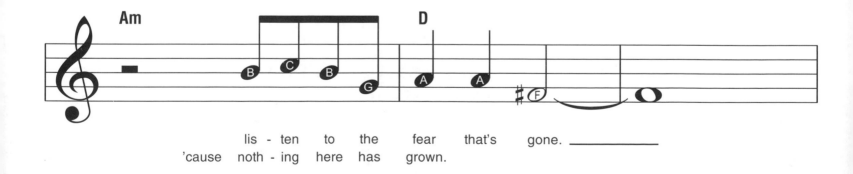

lis - ten to the fear that's gone. _____
'cause noth - ing here has grown.

How Can You Mend a Broken Heart

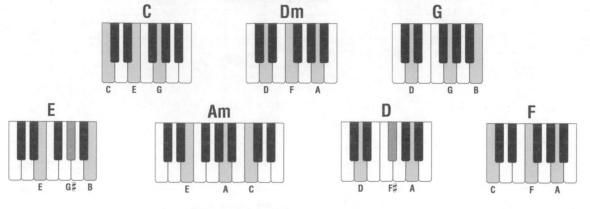

Words and Music by Barry Gibb
and Robin Gibb

Moderately slow Shuffle

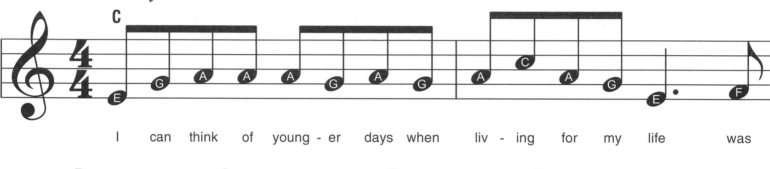

I can think of young-er days when liv-ing for my life was

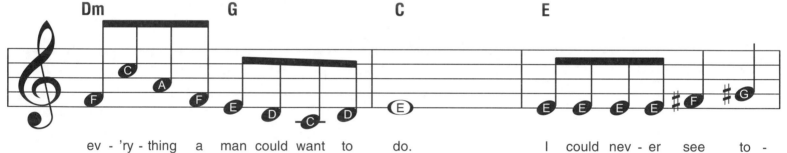

ev-'ry-thing a man could want to do. I could nev-er see to-

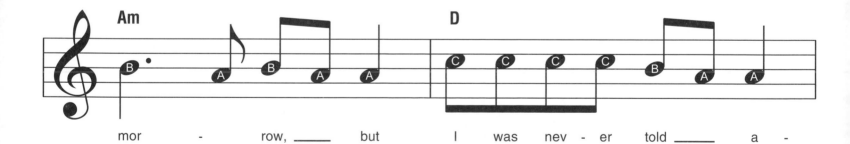

mor - row, _____ but I was nev-er told _____ a-

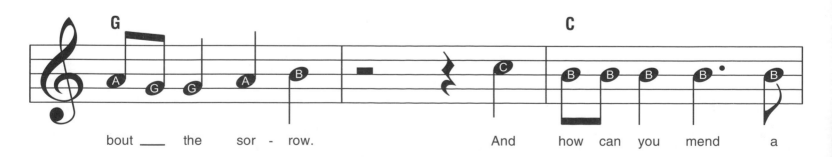

bout _____ the sor-row. And how can you mend a

How Deep Is Your Love
from the Motion Picture SATURDAY NIGHT FEVER

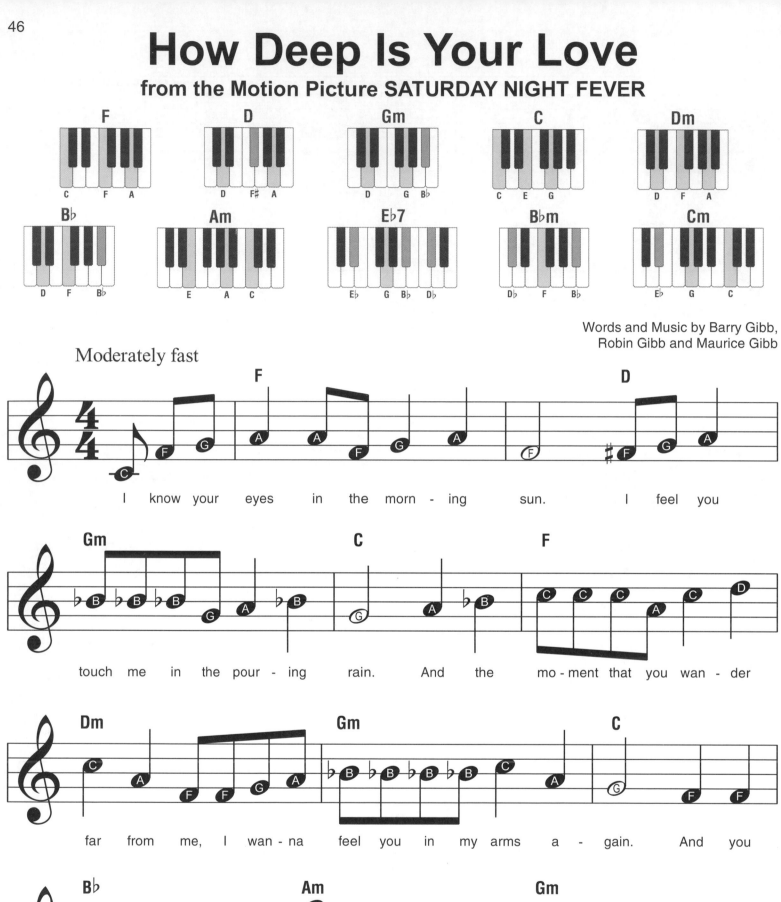

Words and Music by Barry Gibb,
Robin Gibb and Maurice Gibb

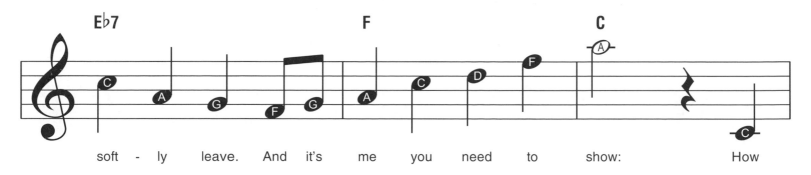

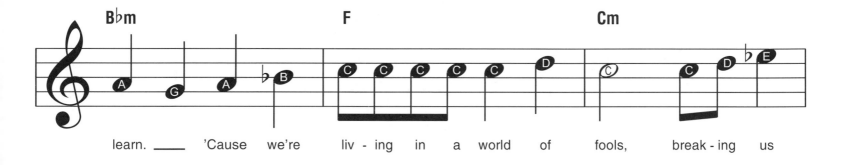

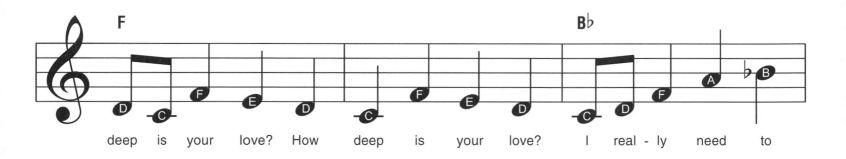

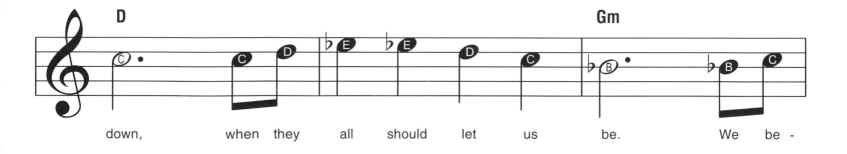

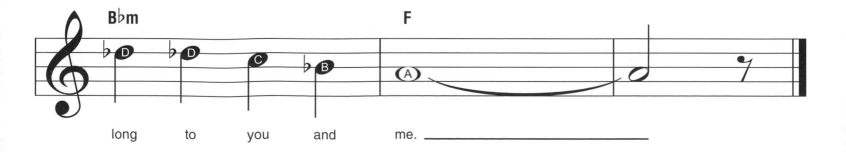

How Sweet It Is
(To Be Loved by You)

Words and Music by Edward Holland,
Lamont Dozier and Brian Holland

49

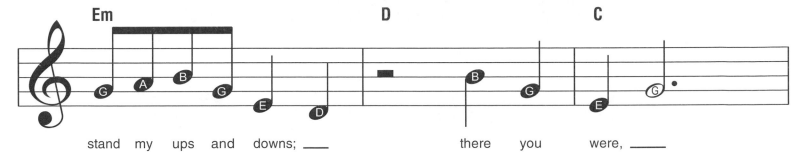

stand my ups and downs; ___ there you were, ___

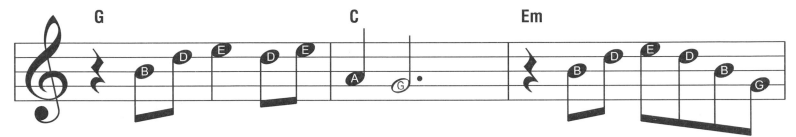

with sweet love and de - vo - tion, deep - ly touch - ing my e -

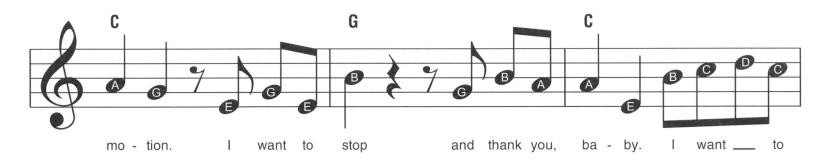

mo - tion. I want to stop and thank you, ba - by. I want ___ to

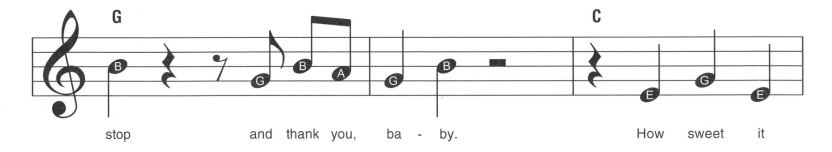

stop and thank you, ba - by. How sweet it

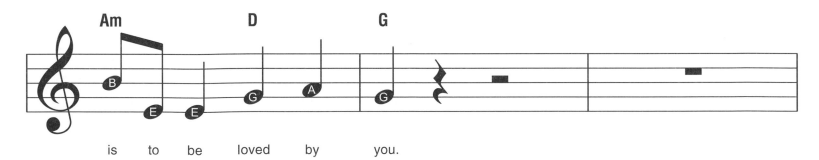

is to be loved by you.

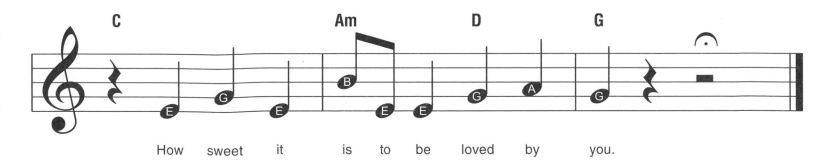

How sweet it is to be loved by you.

I Can See Clearly Now

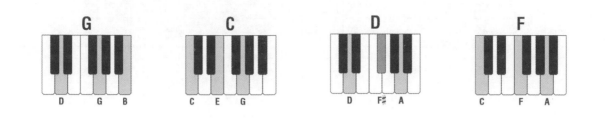

Words and Music by
Johnny Nash

Happily

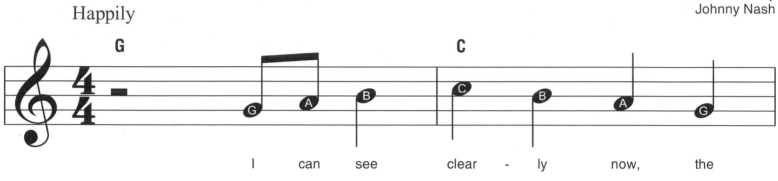

I can see clear - ly now, the

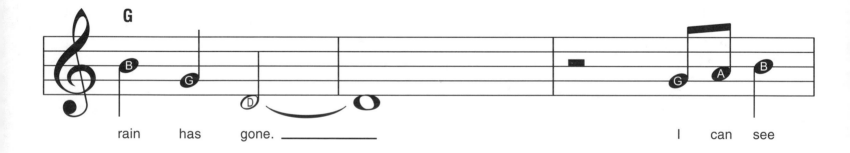

rain has gone. _____   I can see

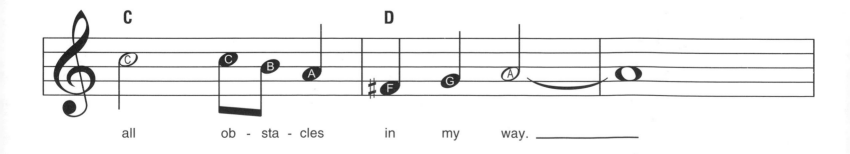

all ob - sta - cles in my way. _____

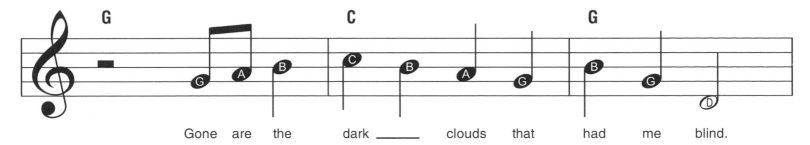

Gone are the dark _____ clouds that had me blind.

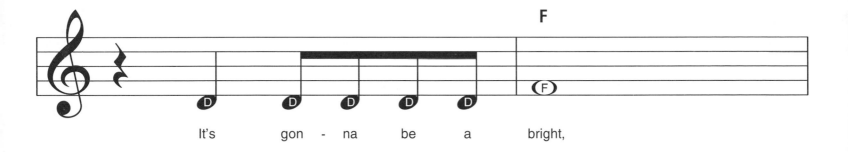

It's gon - na be a bright,

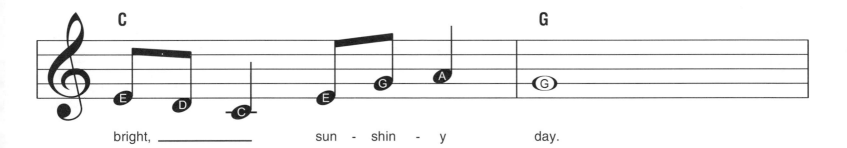

bright, _____ sun - shin - y day.

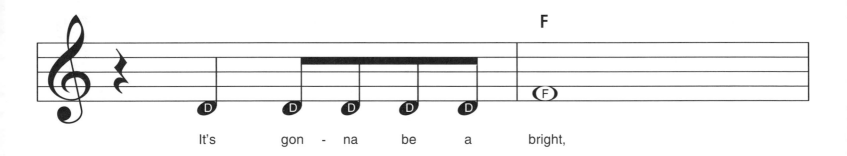

It's gon - na be a bright,

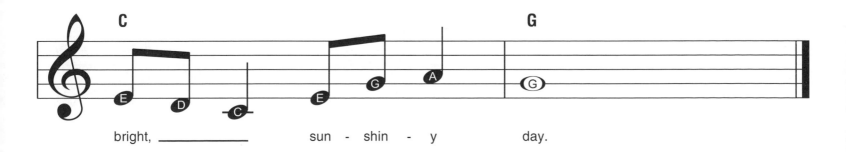

bright, _____ sun - shin - y day.

I Can't Make You Love Me

Words and Music by Mike Reid
and Allen Shamblin

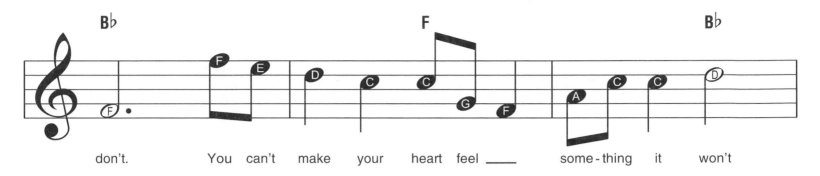

don't. You can't make your heart feel ____ some-thing it won't

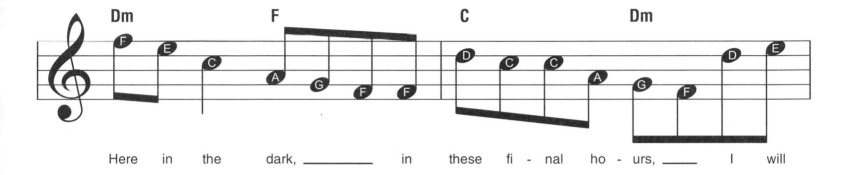

Here in the dark, _____ in these fi-nal ho-urs, ____ I will

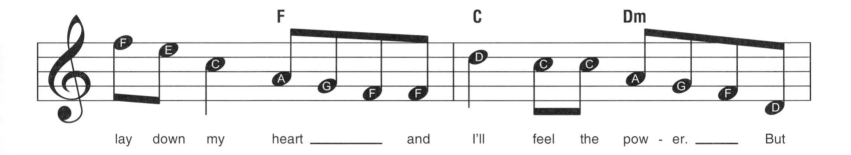

lay down my heart _____ and I'll feel the pow-er. _____ But

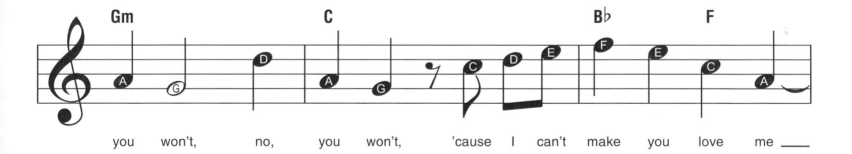

you won't, no, you won't, 'cause I can't make you love me ____

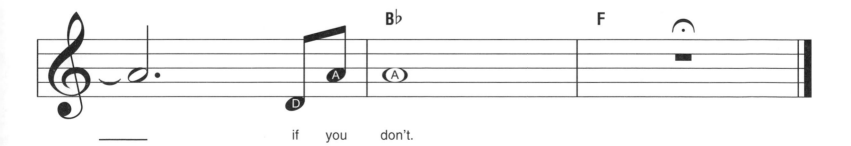

____ if you don't.

I Can't Tell You Why

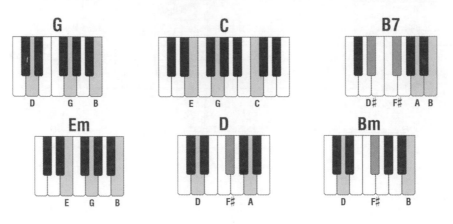

Words and Music by Don Henley,
Glenn Frey and Timothy B. Schmit

Moderately

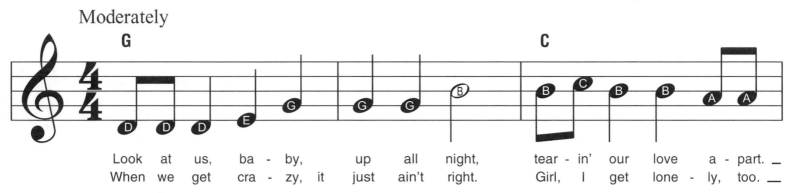

Look at us, ba - by, up all night, tear - in' our love a - part. _
When we get cra - zy, it just ain't right. Girl, I get lone - ly, too. _

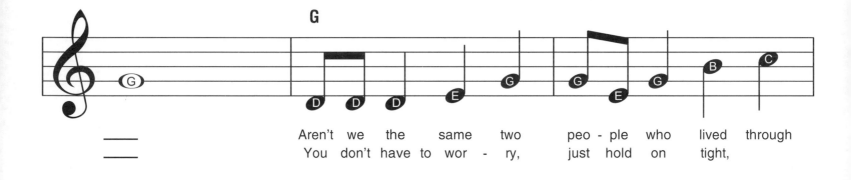

_ Aren't we the same two peo - ple who lived through
_ You don't have to wor - ry, just hold on tight,

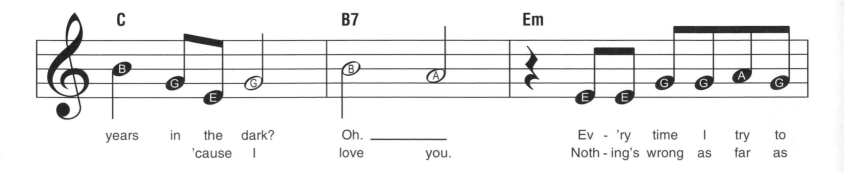

years in the dark? Oh. _____ Ev - 'ry time I try to
'cause I love you. Noth - ing's wrong as far as

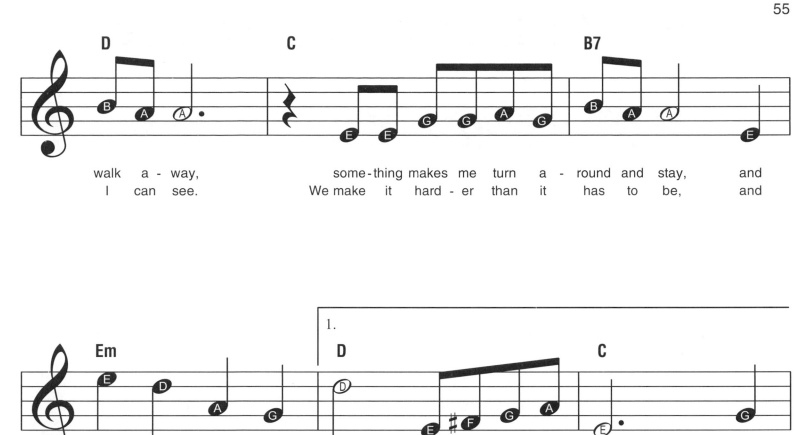

walk a - way,
I can see.

some - thing makes me turn a - round and stay, and
We make it hard - er than it has to be, and

I can't tell you why. *(Instrumental)*
I can't tell you

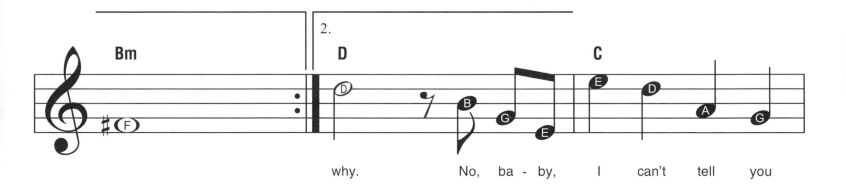

why.   No, ba - by, I can't tell you

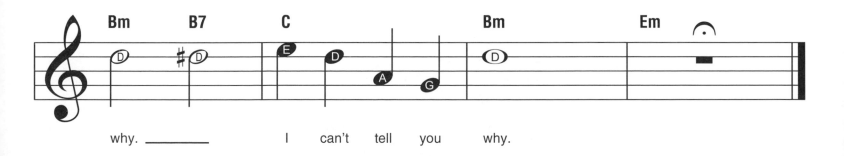

why. _____ I can't tell you why.

I Just Called to Say I Love You

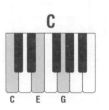 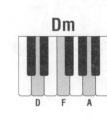 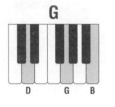 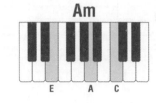

Words and Music by
Stevie Wonder

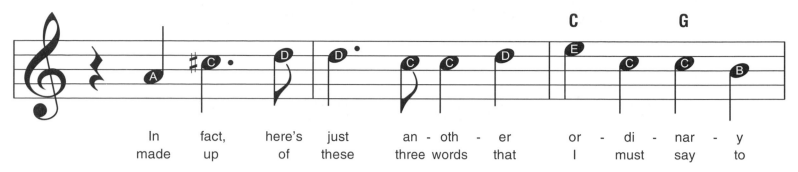

In fact, here's just an - oth - er or - di - nar - y
made up of these three words that I must say to

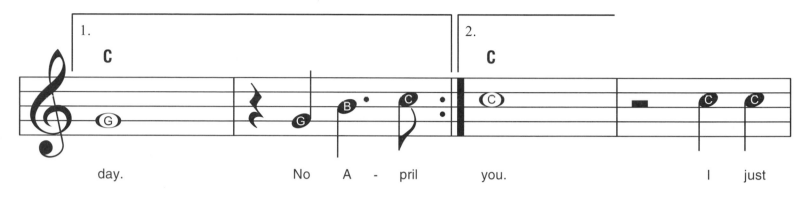

day. No A - pril you. I just

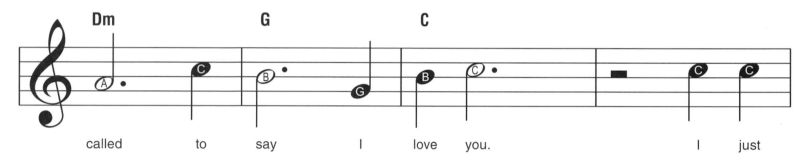

called to say I love you. I just

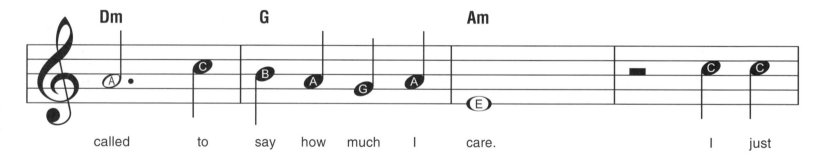

called to say how much I care. I just

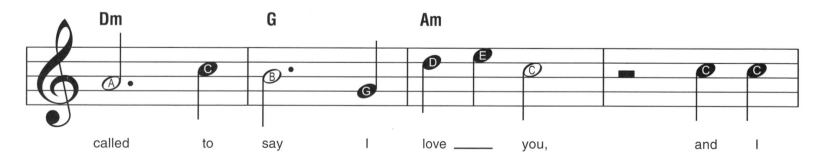

called to say I love _____ you, and I

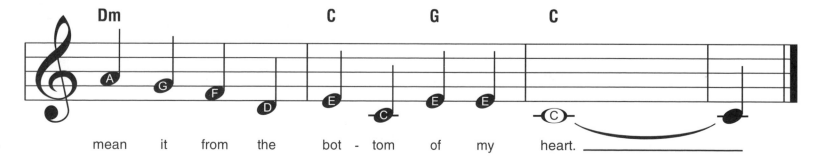

mean it from the bot - tom of my heart. _____

I Will Always Love You

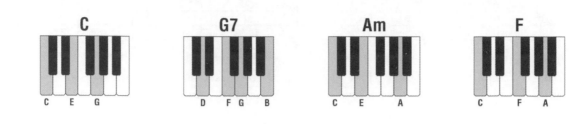

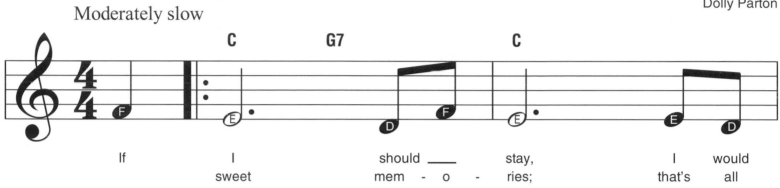

Words and Music by
Dolly Parton

Moderately slow

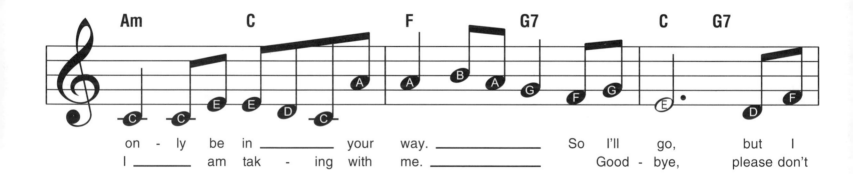

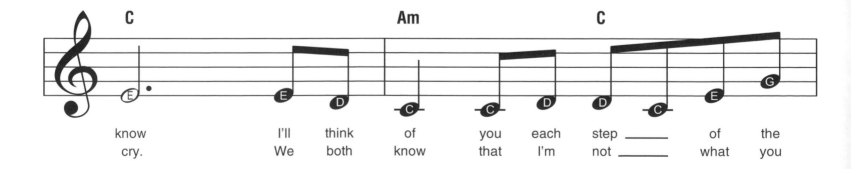

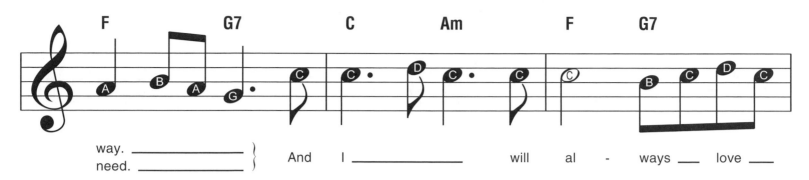

way. _____ }
need. _____ } And I _____ will al - ways ___ love ___

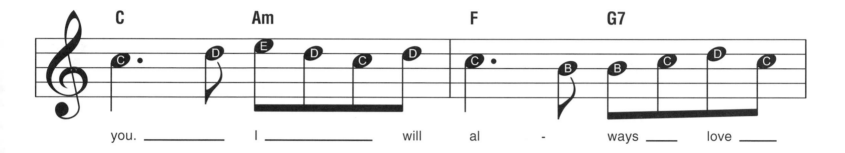

you. _____ I _____ will al - ways ___ love ___

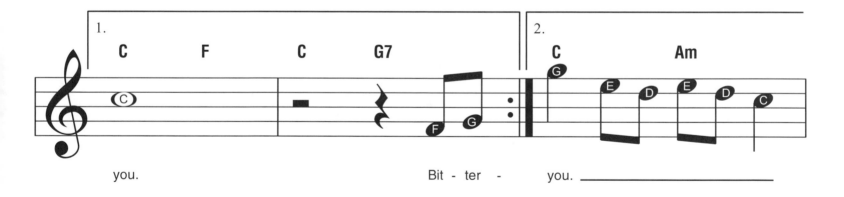

you. Bit - ter - you. _____

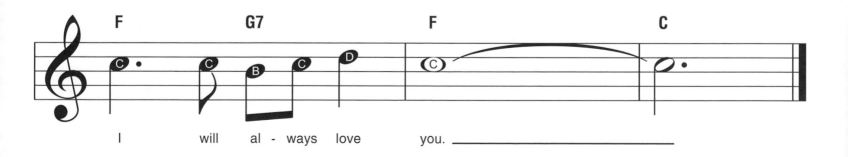

I will al - ways love you. _____

I'm Not in Love

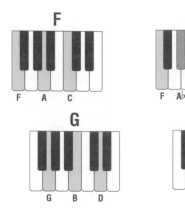
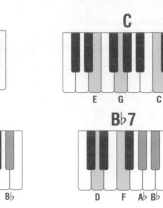
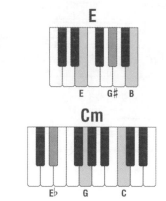
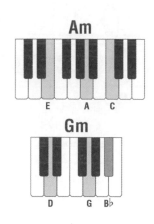

Words and Music by Eric Stewart
and Graham Gouldman

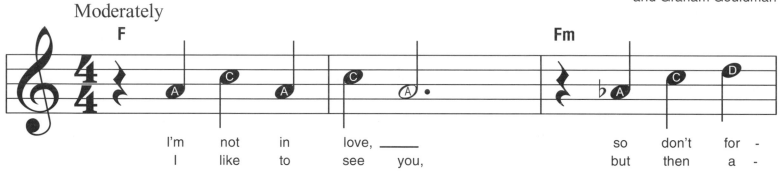

I'm not in love, _____ so don't for -
I like to see you, but then a -

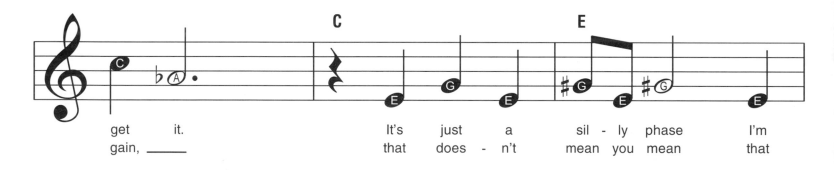

get it. It's just a sil - ly phase I'm
gain, _____ that does - n't mean you mean that

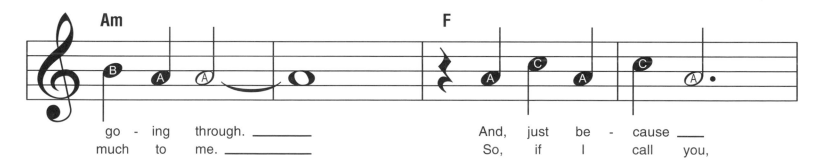

go - ing through. _____ And, just be - cause _____
much to me. _____ So, if I call you,

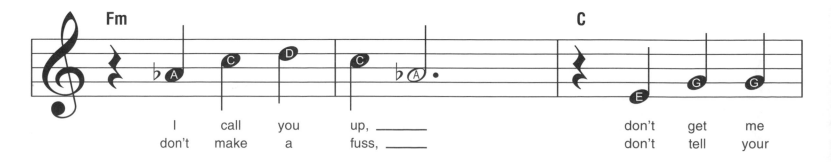

I call you up, _____ don't get me
don't make a fuss, _____ don't tell your

If You Don't Know Me by Now

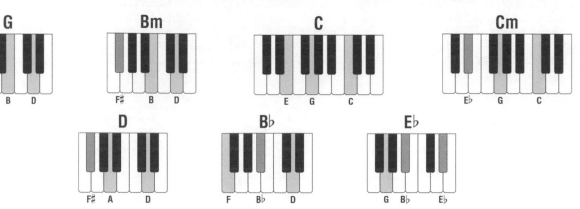

Words and Music by Kenneth Gamble
and Leon Huff

Moderate Shuffle

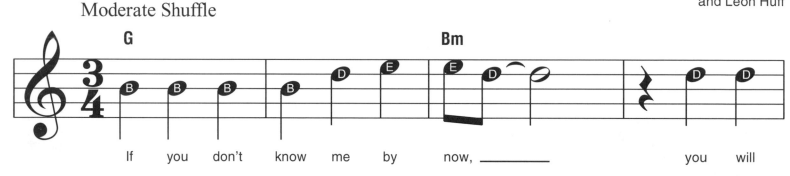

If you don't know me by now, _____ you will

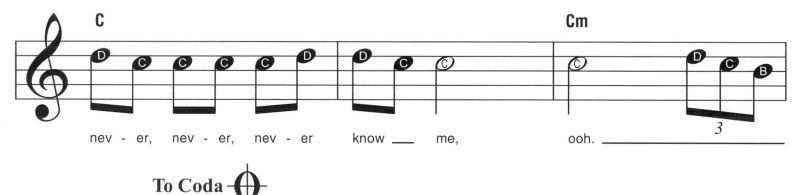

nev - er, nev - er, nev - er know ___ me, ooh. _____

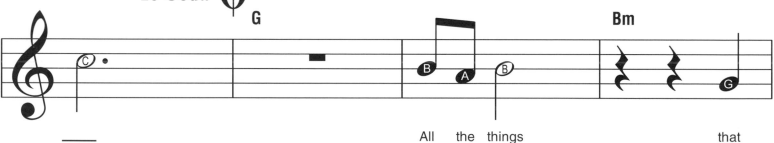

___ All the things that

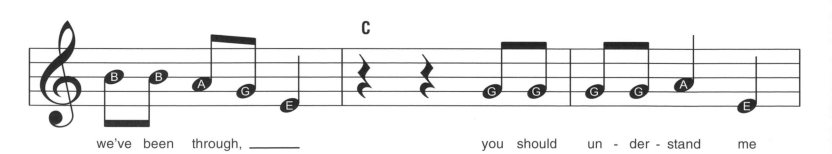

we've been through, _____ you should un - der - stand me

Imagine

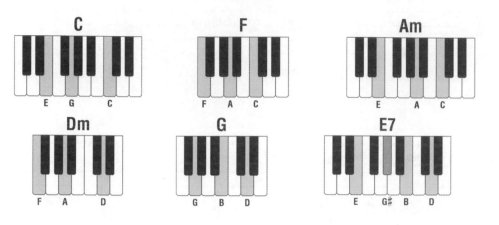

Words and Music by
John Lennon

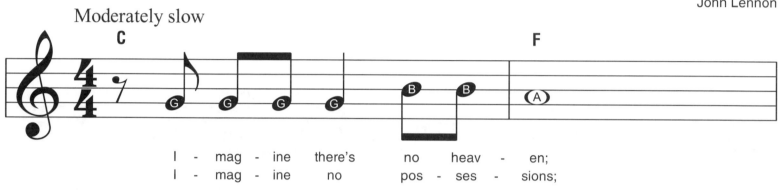

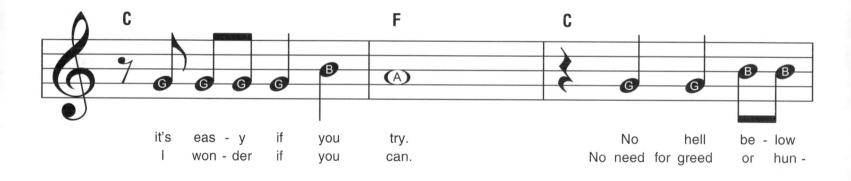

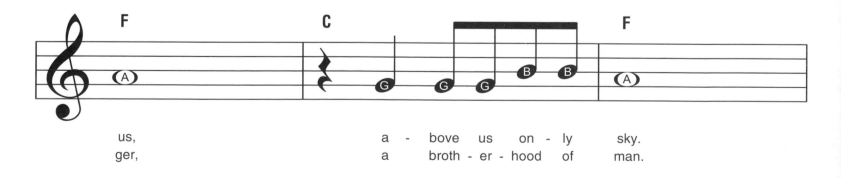

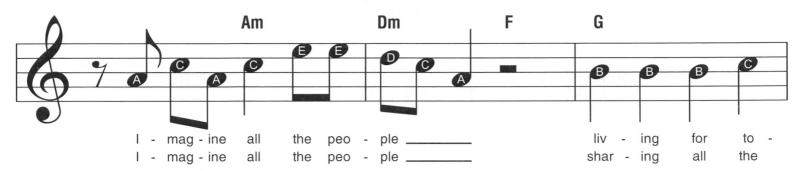

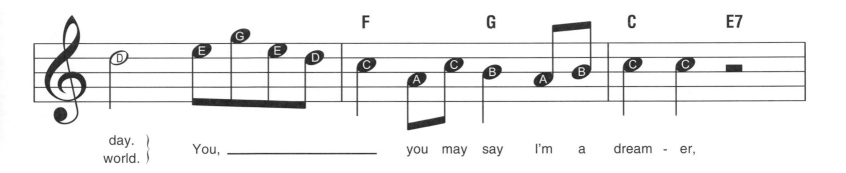

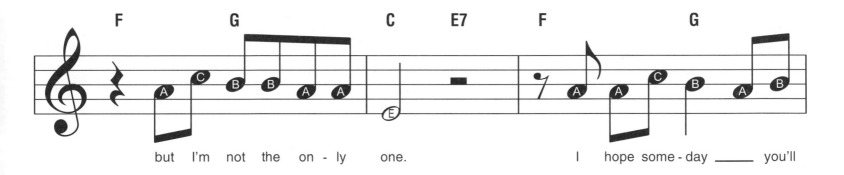

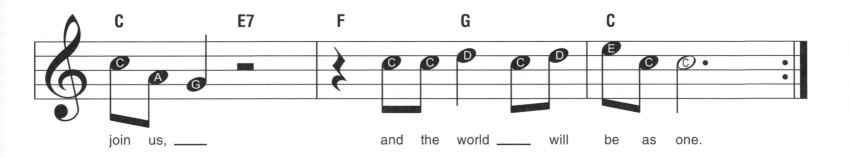

Isn't She Lovely

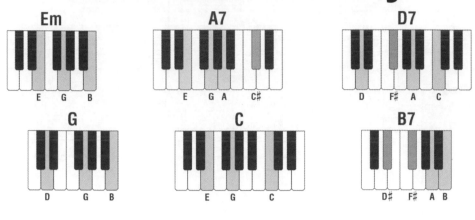

Words and Music by
Stevie Wonder

Man in the Mirror

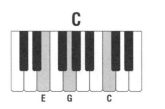
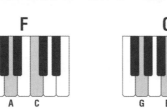
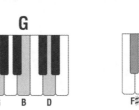
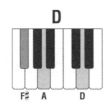
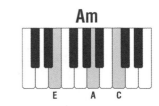

Words and Music by Glen Ballard
and Siedah Garrett

I'm start - ing with the man ____ in the mir - ror.

I'm ask - ing him to change _ his ways. ____ And no mes-sage could have

been an - y clear - er: if you wan - na make the world a bet - ter place, take a

look at your - self and then make a change. _____

Na na na, na na na, na na ____ na na. ____

It's Too Late

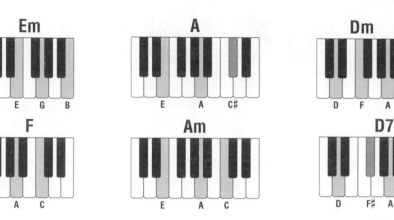
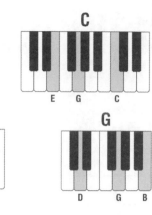

Words and Music by Carole King
and Toni Stern

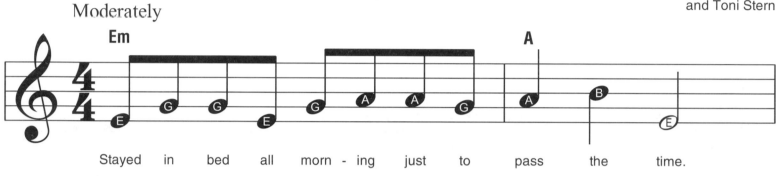

Stayed in bed all morn-ing just to pass the time.

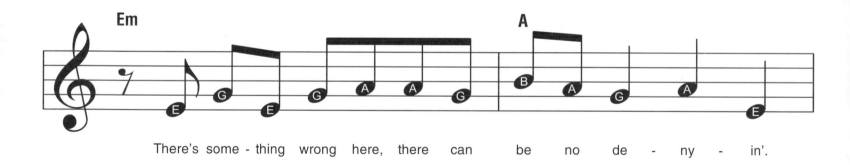

There's some-thing wrong here, there can be no de-ny-in'.

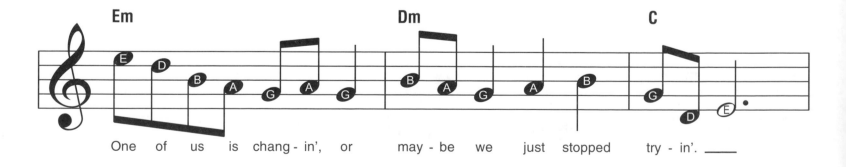

One of us is chang-in', or may-be we just stopped try-in'. ____

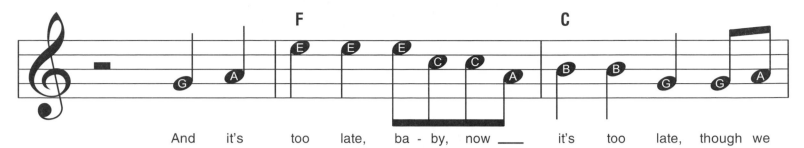

And it's too late, ba - by, now ___ it's too late, though we

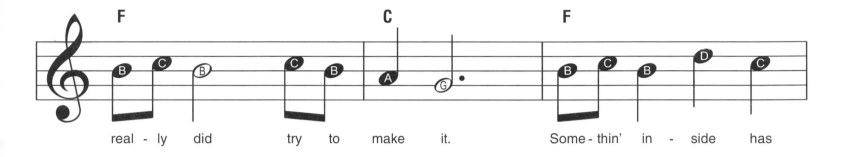

real - ly did try to make it. Some - thin' in - side has

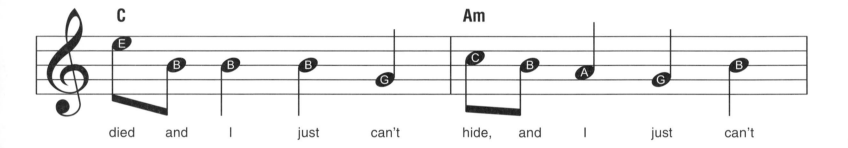

died and I just can't hide, and I just can't

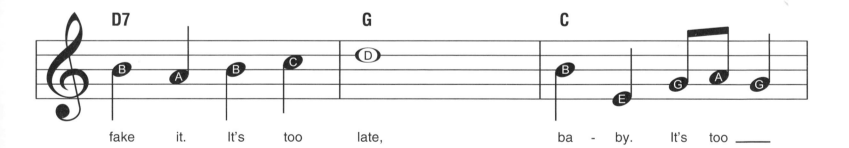

fake it. It's too late, ba - by. It's too ___

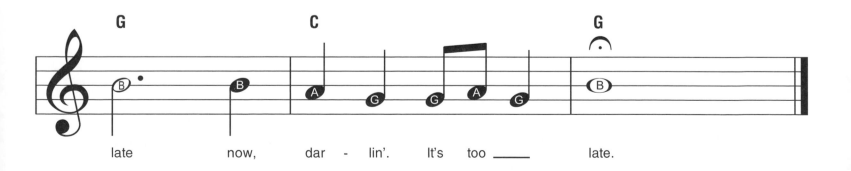

late now, dar - lin'. It's too ___ late.

Just My Imagination
(Running Away with Me)

Words and Music by Norman Whitfield
and Barrett Strong

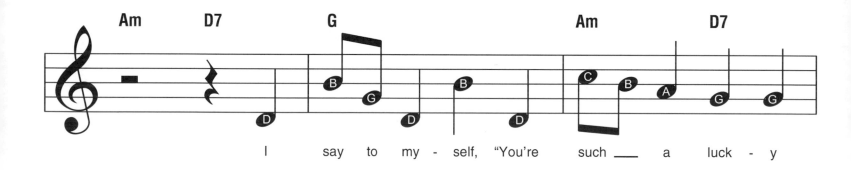

Each day through my win-dow, I watch her as she pass-es by. _____

I say to my-self, "You're such ___ a luck-y

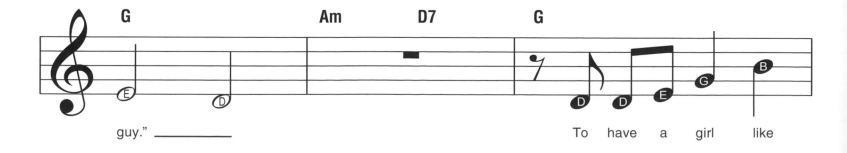

guy." _____ To have a girl like

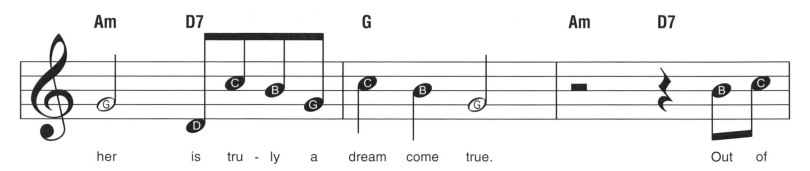

her is tru - ly a dream come true. Out of

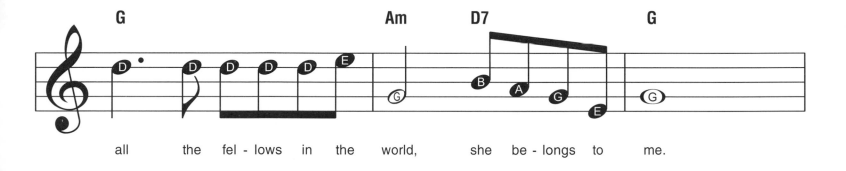

all the fel - lows in the world, she be - longs to me.

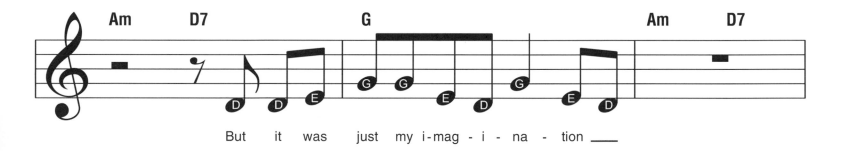

But it was just my i-mag - i - na - tion ___

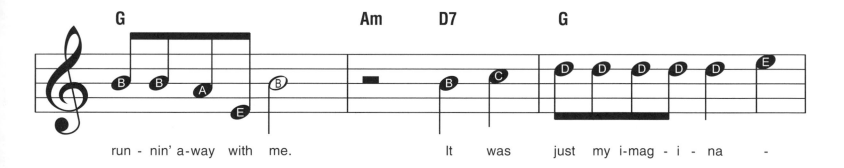

run - nin' a-way with me. It was just my i-mag - i - na -

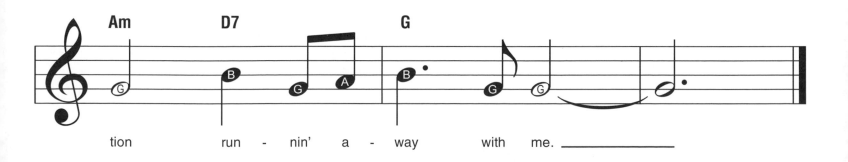

tion run - nin' a - way with me. ___

Just the Way You Are

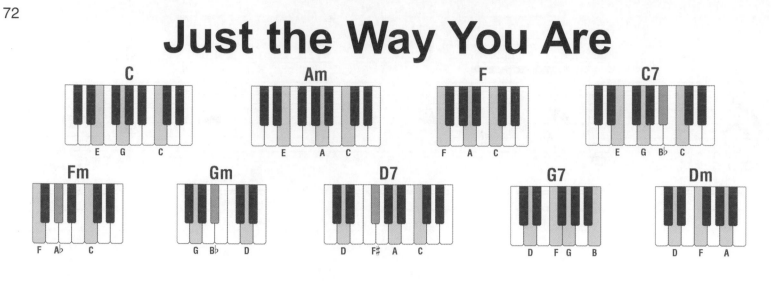

Words and Music by
Billy Joel

Moderately fast

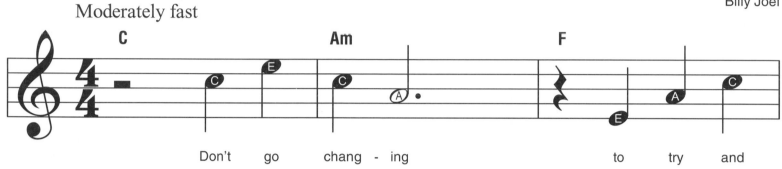

Don't go chang-ing to try and

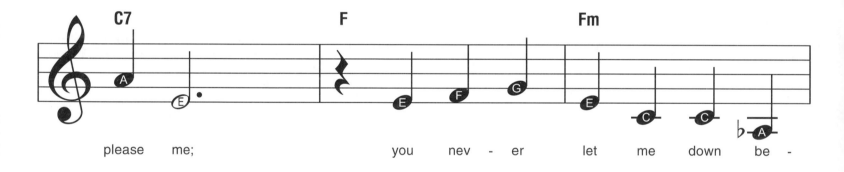

please me; you nev-er let me down be-

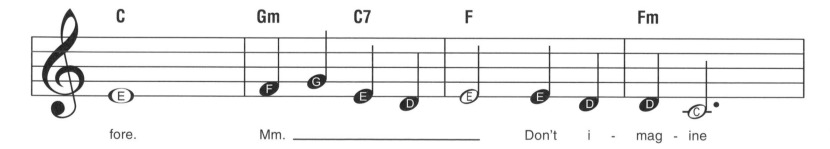

fore. Mm. _____ Don't i-mag-ine

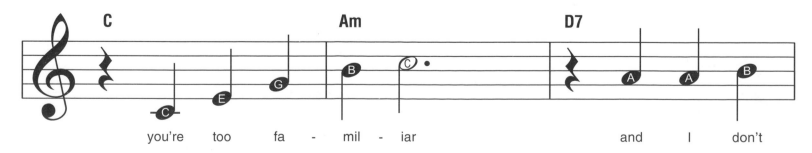

you're too fa-mil-iar and I don't

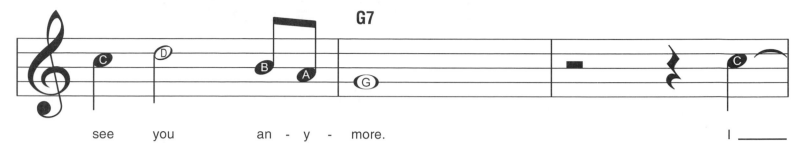

see you an - y - more. I ____

____ would not leave you in times of

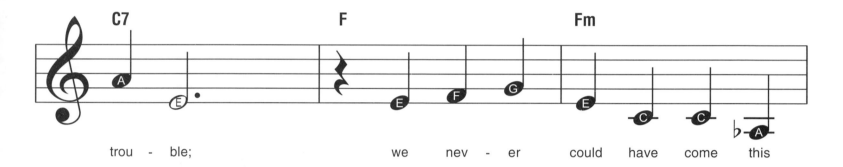

trou - ble; we nev - er could have come this

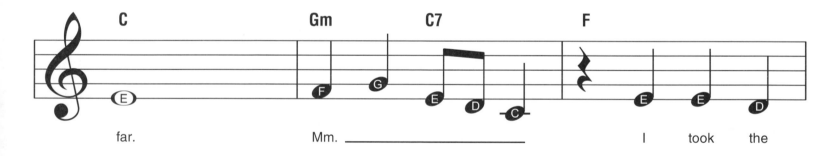

far. Mm. ____ I took the

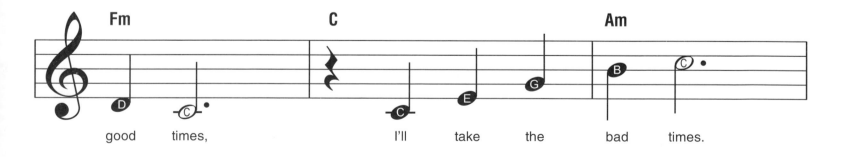

good times, I'll take the bad times.

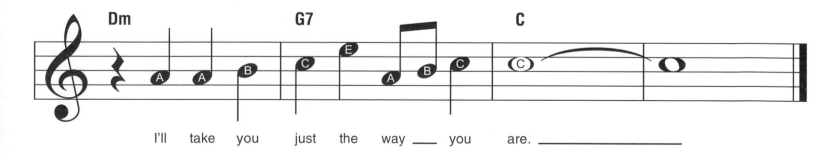

I'll take you just the way ___ you are. ____

Knockin' on Heaven's Door

Lean on Me

Words and Music by
Bill Withers

To Coda

For it won't be long _____ till I'm gon-na need _____ some-bod-y to

lean _____ on. You just call on me, broth - er, when

you need a hand. We all need some-bod-y to lean _____ on. I just

might have a prob - lem that you'll un-der-stand. We all need some-bod-y to

D.S. al Coda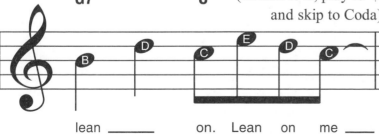
(Return to ⅖, play to ⊕ and skip to Coda)

CODA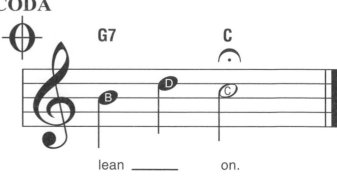

lean _____ on. Lean on me ___

lean _____ on.

The Look of Love

from CASINO ROYALE

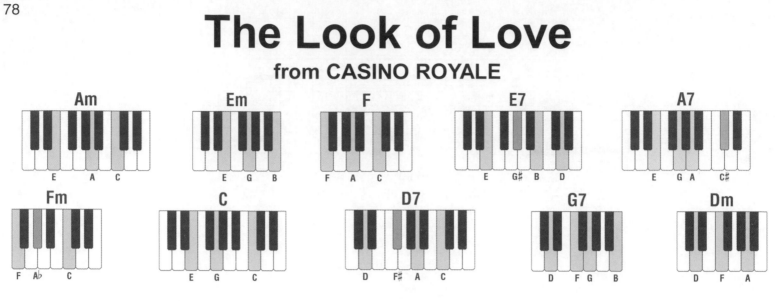

Words and Music by Hal David
and Burt Bacharach

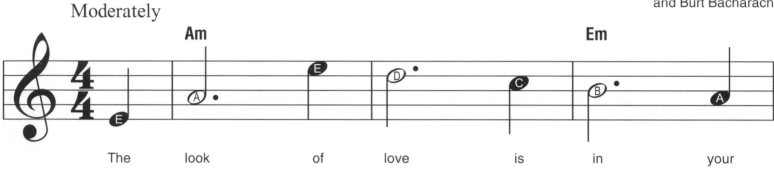

The look of love is in your

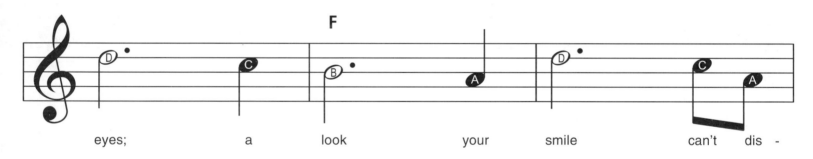

eyes; a look your smile can't dis-

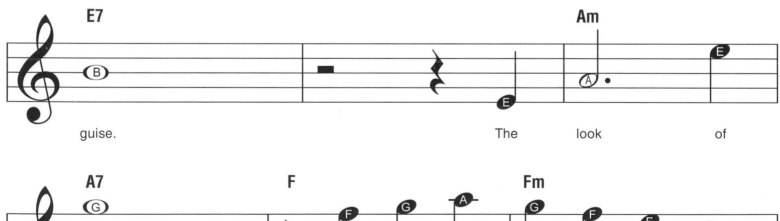

guise. The look of

love, it's say - ing so much more than just

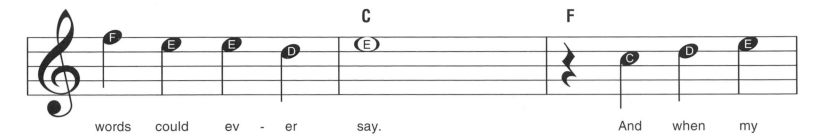

words could ev - er say.   And when my

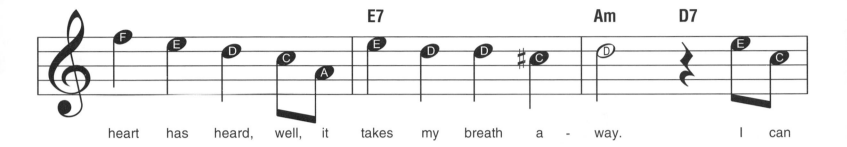

heart has heard, well, it takes my breath a - way.   I can

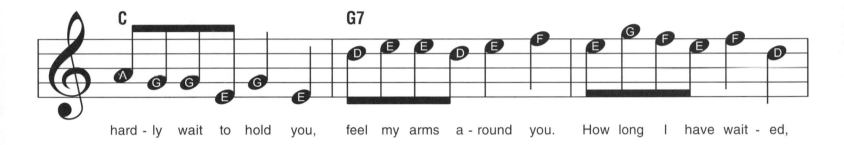

hard - ly wait to hold you, feel my arms a - round you. How long I have wait - ed,

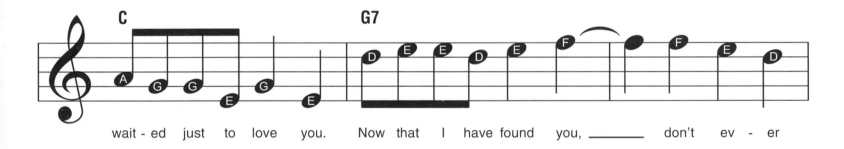

wait - ed just to love you. Now that I have found you, _____ don't ev - er

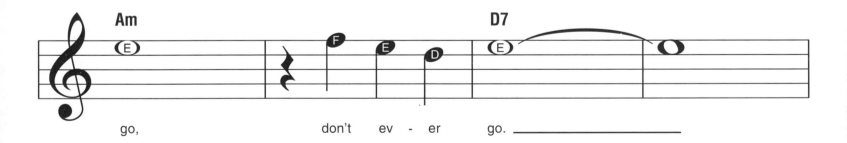

go,   don't ev - er go. _____

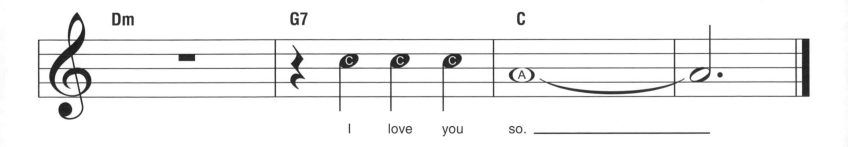

I love you so. _____

Mack the Knife
from THE THREEPENNY OPERA

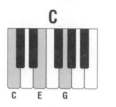  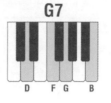 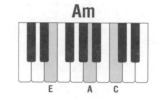

English Words by Marc Blitzstein
Original German Words by Bert Brecht
Music by Kurt Weill

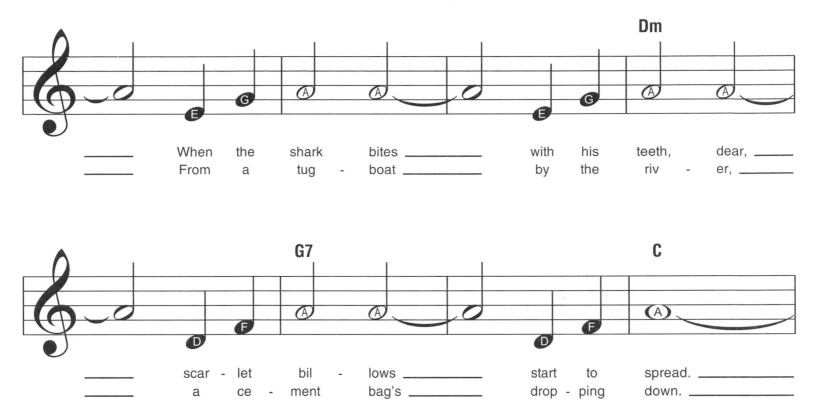

When the shark bites _____ with his teeth, dear, _____
From a tug - boat _____ by the riv - er, _____

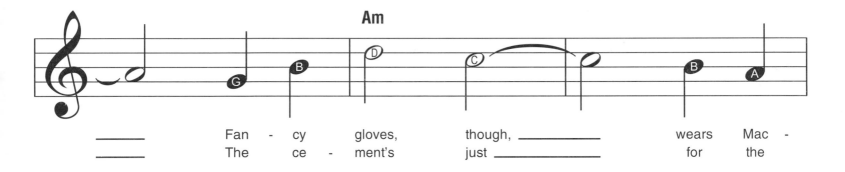

_____ scar - let bil - lows _____ start to spread. _____
_____ a ce - ment bag's _____ drop - ping down. _____

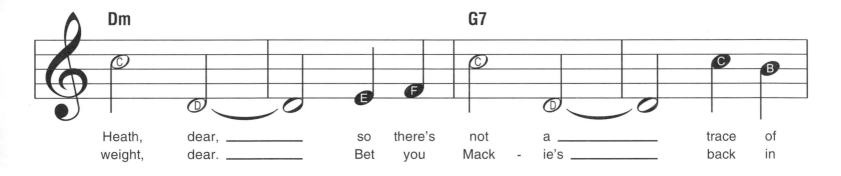

_____ Fan - cy gloves, though, _____ wears Mac -
_____ The ce - ment's just _____ for the

Heath, dear, _____ so there's not a _____ trace of
weight, dear. _____ Bet you Mack - ie's _____ back in

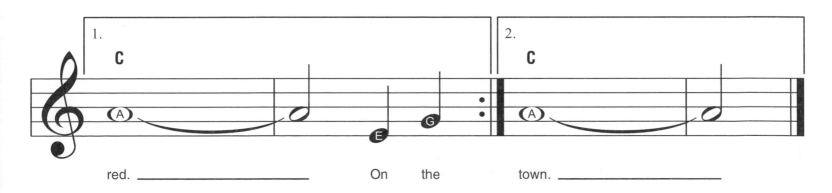

red. _____ On the town. _____

My Heart Will Go On
(Love Theme from 'Titanic')
from the Paramount and Twentieth Century Fox Motion Picture TITANIC

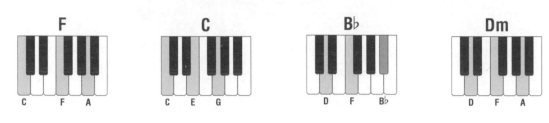

Music by James Horner
Lyric by Will Jennings

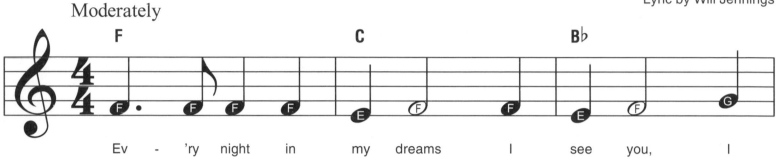

Moderately

Ev - 'ry night in my dreams I see you, I

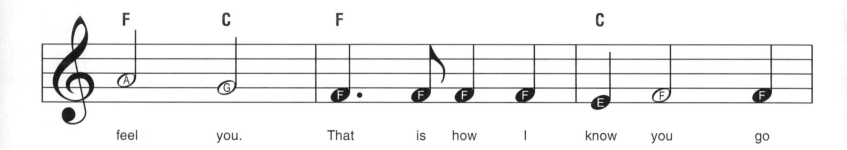

feel you. That is how I know you go

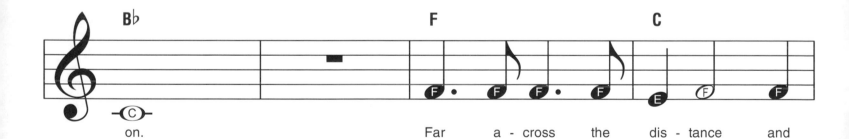

on. Far a - cross the dis - tance and

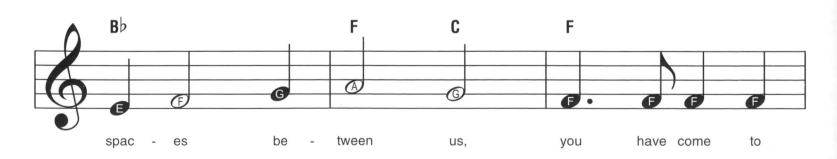

spac - es be - tween us, you have come to

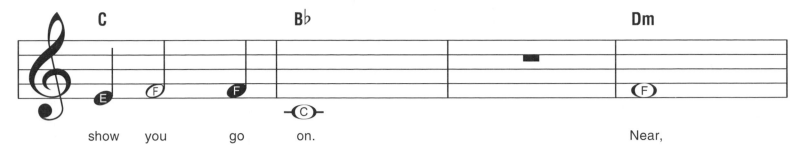

show you go on. Near,

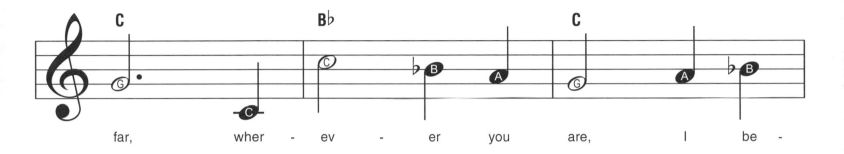

far, wher - ev - er you are, I be -

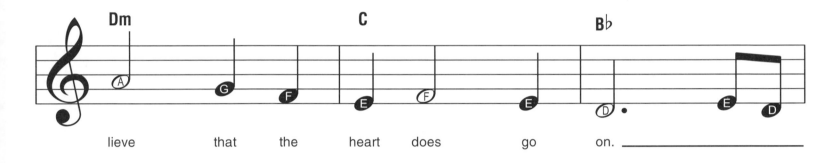

lieve that the heart does go on. _____

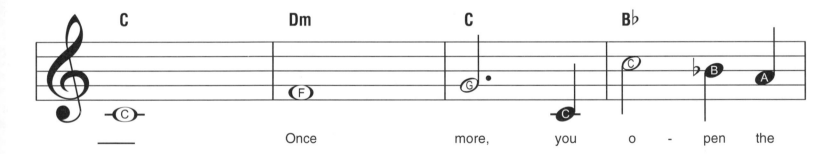

_____ Once more, you o - pen the

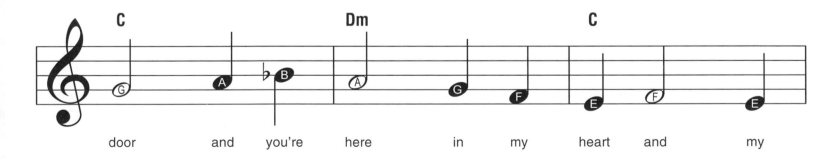

door and you're here in my heart and my

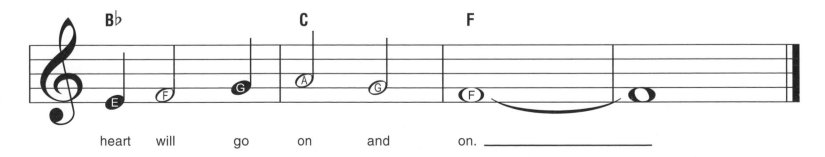

heart will go on and on. _____

On Broadway

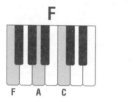
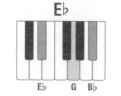
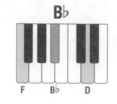
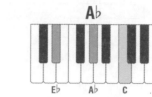
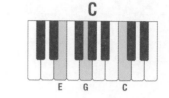

Words and Music by Barry Mann,
Cynthia Weil, Mike Stoller
and Jerry Leiber

Moderately

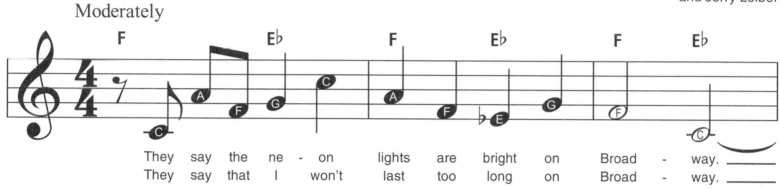

They say the ne - on lights are bright on Broad - way. _____
They say that I won't last too long on Broad - way. _____

_____ They say there's al - ways mag - ic in the
_____ I'll catch a Grey - hound bus for home, they

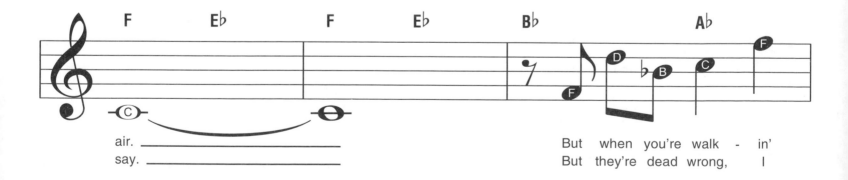

air. _____
say. _____

But when you're walk - in'
But they're dead wrong, I

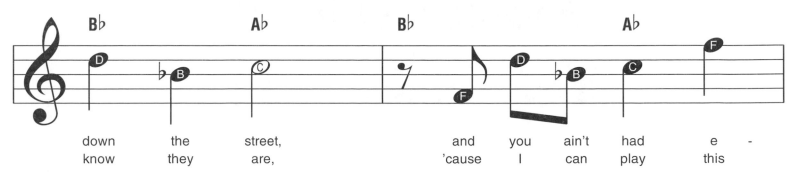

down   the   street,   and   you   ain't   had   e -
know   they   are,   'cause   I   can   had   play   this

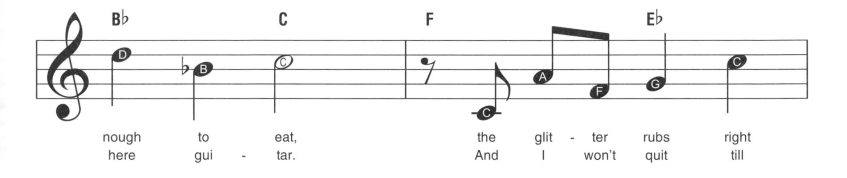

nough   to   eat,   the   glit - ter   rubs   right
here   to   gui - tar.   And   I   won't   quit   right   till

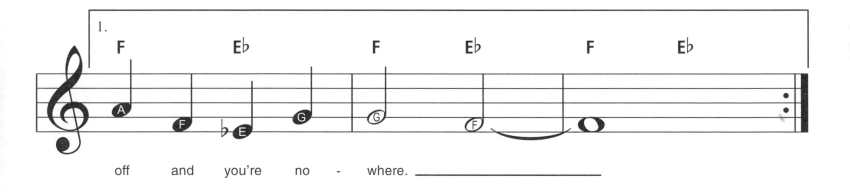

1.

off   and   you're   no - where. _____

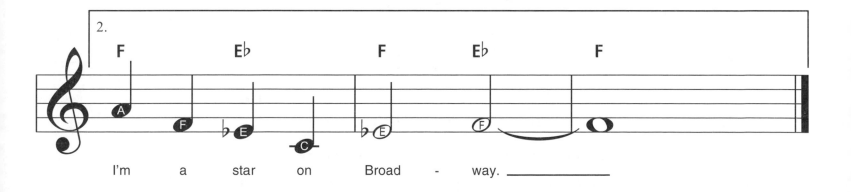

2.

I'm   a   star   on   Broad - way. _____

People Get Ready

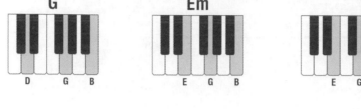

Words and Music by
Curtis Mayfield

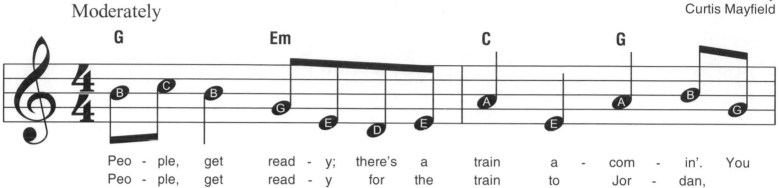

Peo - ple, get read - y; there's a train a - com - in'. You
Peo - ple, get read - y for the train to Jor - dan,

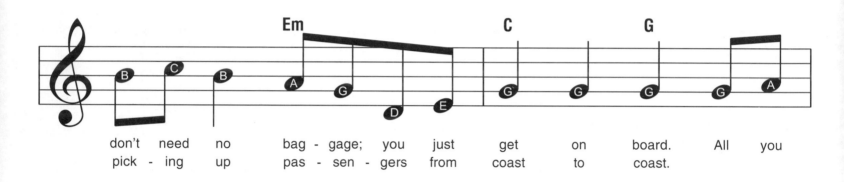

don't need no bag - gage; you just get on board. All you
pick - ing up pas - sen - gers just from coast to coast.

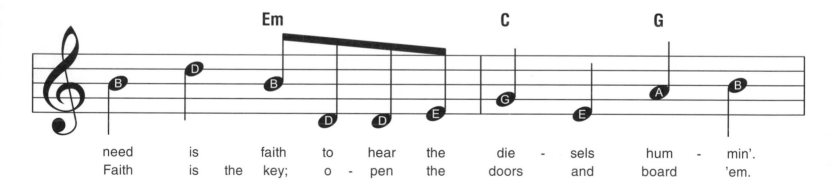

need is faith to hear the die - sels hum - min'.
Faith is the key; o - pen the doors and board 'em.

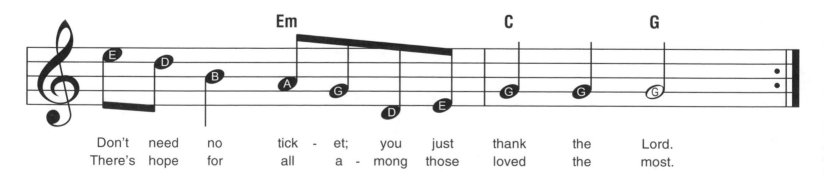

Don't need no tick - et; you just thank the Lord.
There's hope for all a - mong those loved the most.

Signed, Sealed, Delivered I'm Yours

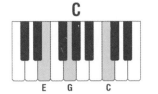
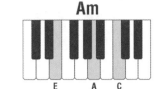
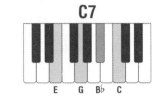
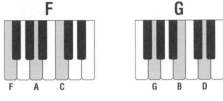

Words and Music by Stevie Wonder,
Syreeta Wright, Lee Garrett
and Lula Mae Hardaway

With energy

Like a fool, I went and stayed too long. _____
Then that time I went and said good - bye. _____

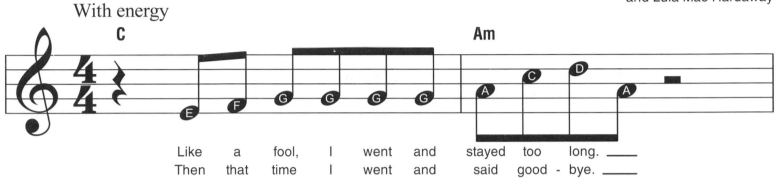

Now I'm won - d'ring if your love's still strong. }
Now I'm back and not a - shamed to cry. } Ooh,

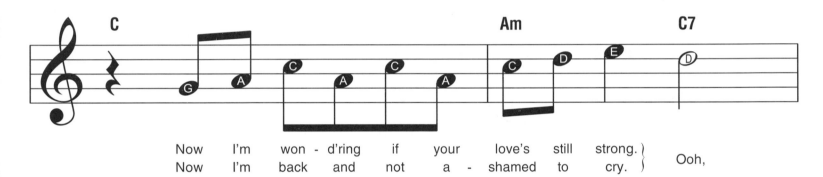

ba - by, here I am. Signed, sealed, de - liv - ered; I'm yours.

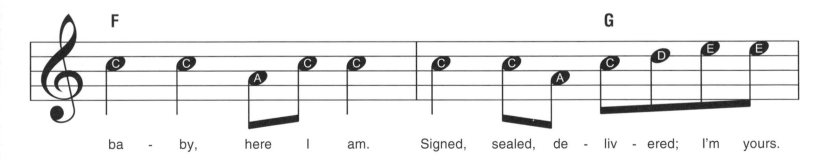

(Instrumental)

Pure Imagination
from WILLY WONKA AND THE CHOCOLATE FACTORY

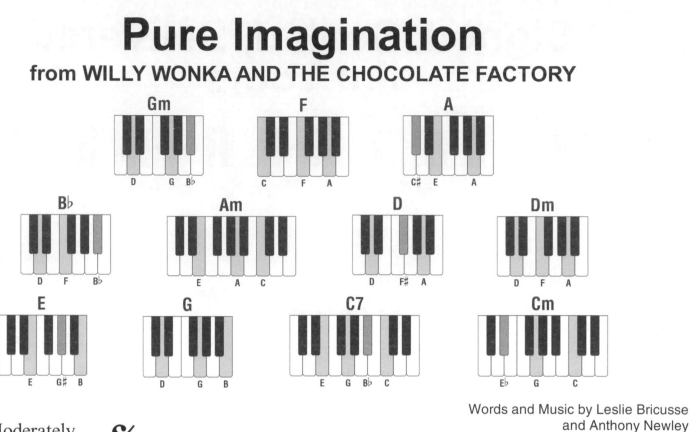

Words and Music by Leslie Bricusse
and Anthony Newley

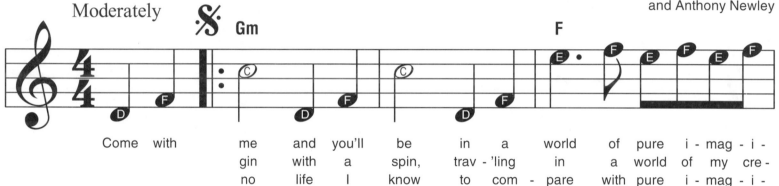

Come with me and you'll be in a world of pure i-mag-i-
gin with a spin, trav-'ling in a world of my cre-
no life I know to com-pare with pure i-mag-i-

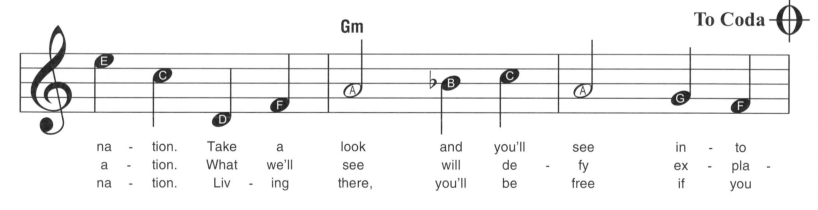

na - tion. Take a look and you'll see in - to
a - tion. What we'll see will de - fy ex - pla -
na - tion. Liv - ing there, you'll be free if you

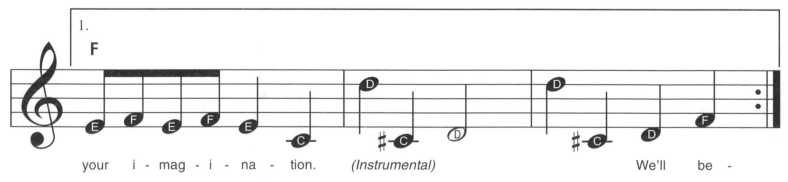

your i-mag-i-na-tion. (Instrumental) We'll be-

na - tion. _____ If you want to view

par - a - dise, sim - ply look a - round and view it.

An - y - thing you want to, do it. Want to change the world? There's

D.S. al Coda
(Return to 𝄋, play to ⊕
and skip to Coda)

CODA

noth - ing to it! _____ There is

tru - ly

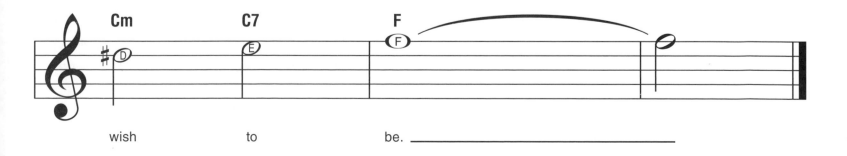

wish to be. _____

Red, Red Wine

Words and Music by
Neil Diamond

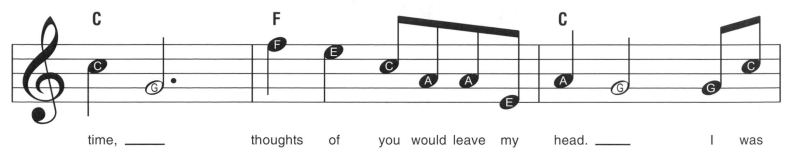

time, _____ thoughts of you would leave my head. _____ I was

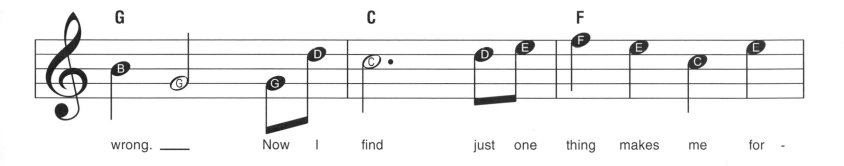

wrong. ____ Now I find just one thing makes me for -

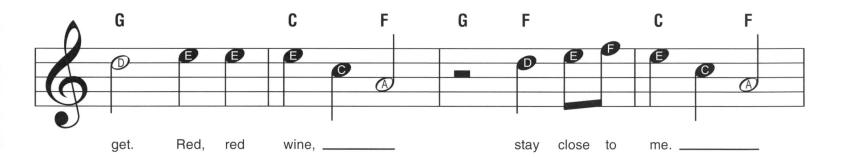

get. Red, red wine, _____ stay close to me. _____

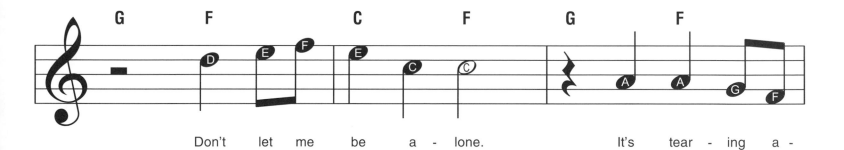

Don't let me be a - lone. It's tear - ing a -

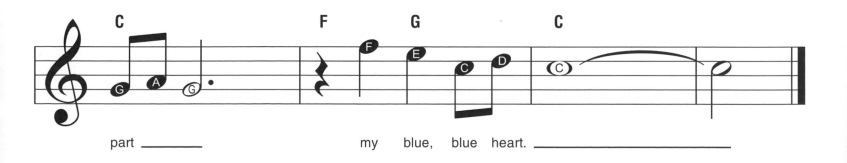

part _____ my blue, blue heart. _____

Right Here Waiting

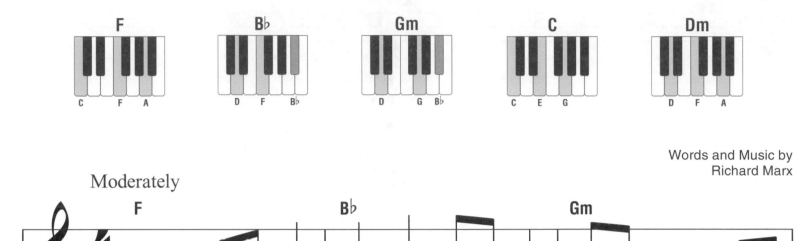

Words and Music by
Richard Marx

Moderately

O - ceans a - part, ____ day af - ter day, _____ and I

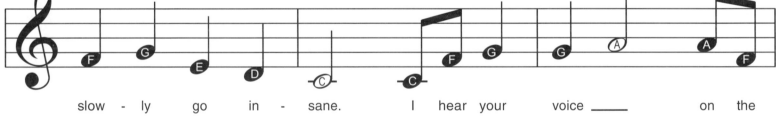

slow - ly go in - sane. I hear your voice ____ on the

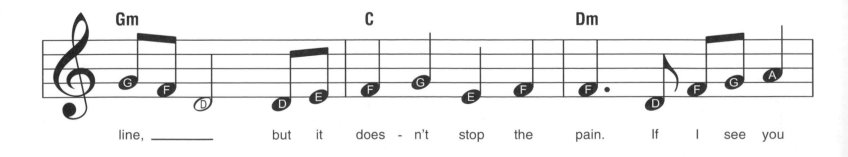

line, _____ but it does - n't stop the pain. If I see you

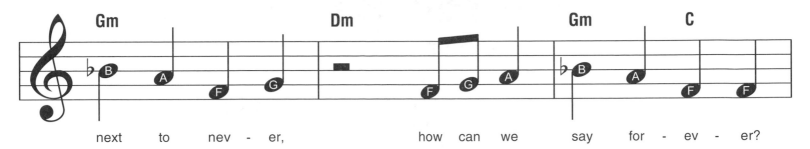

next to nev - er, how can we say for - ev - er?

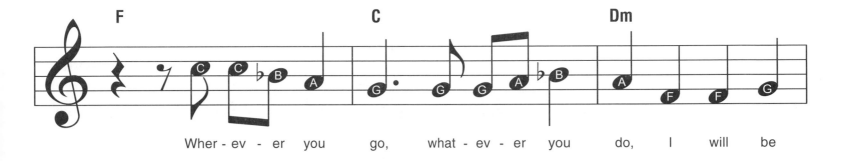

Wher - ev - er you go, what - ev - er you do, I will be

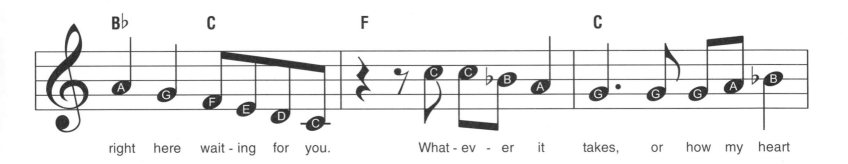

right here wait - ing for you. What - ev - er it takes, or how my heart

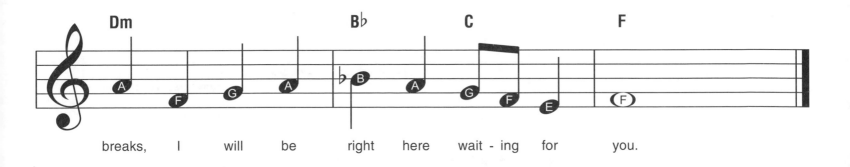

breaks, I will be right here wait - ing for you.

Say You, Say Me

from the Motion Picture WHITE NIGHTS

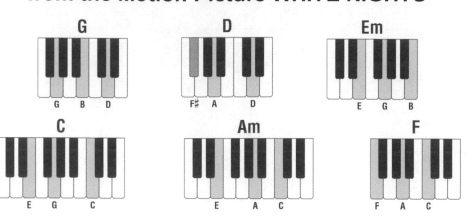

Words and Music by
Lionel Richie

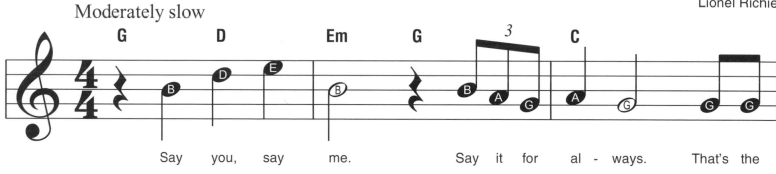

Say you, say me. Say it for al - ways. That's the

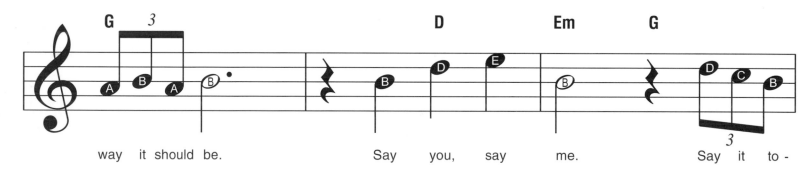

way it should be. Say you, say me. Say it to-

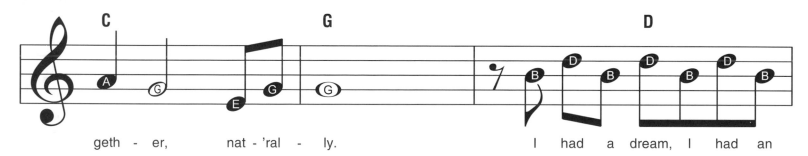

geth - er, nat - 'ral - ly. I had a dream, I had an

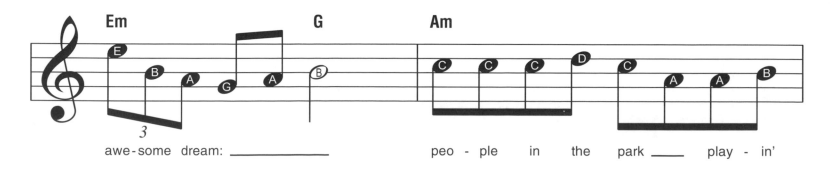

awe-some dream: _____ peo - ple in the park _____ play - in'

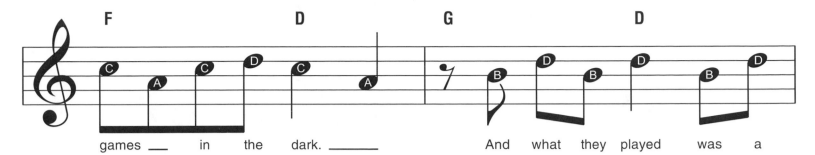

games ___ in the dark. _____ And what they played was a

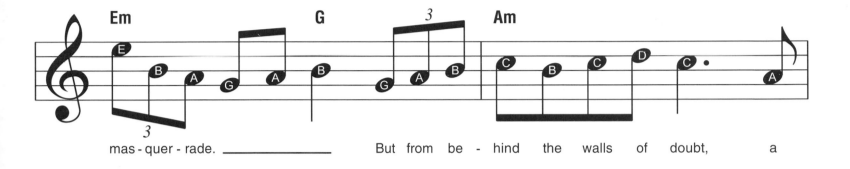

mas-quer-rade. _____ But from be-hind the walls of doubt, a

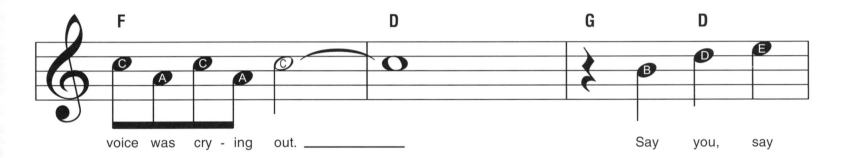

voice was cry-ing out. _____ Say you, say

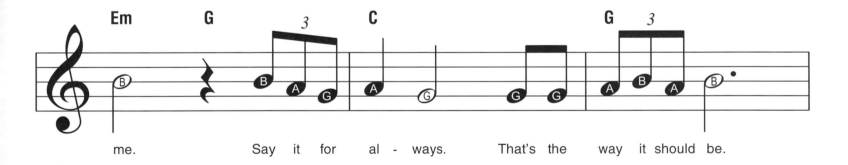

me. Say it for al-ways. That's the way it should be.

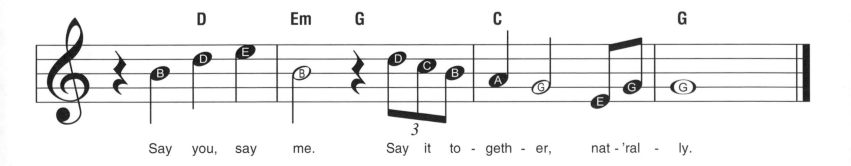

Say you, say me. Say it to-geth-er, nat-'ral-ly.

Stand by Me

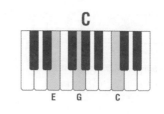

Words and Music by Jerry Leiber,
Mike Stoller and Ben E. King

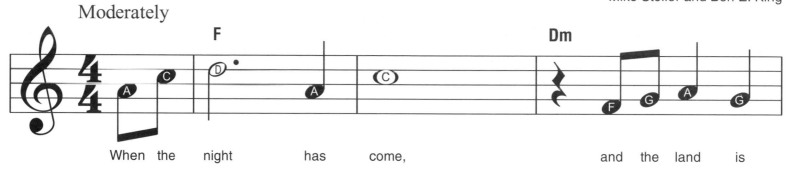

When the night has come, and the land is

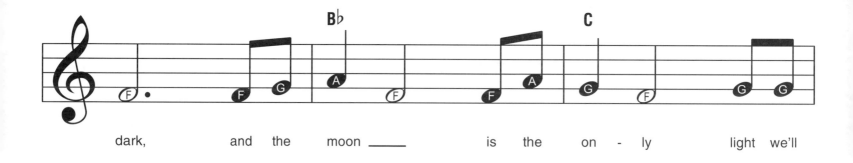

dark, and the moon _____ is the on - ly light we'll

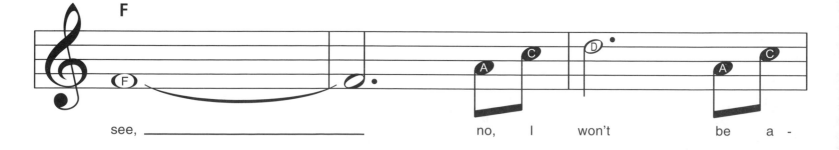

see, _____ no, I won't be a -

Sunny

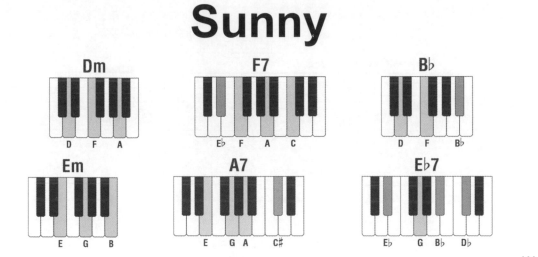

Words and Music by
Bobby Hebb

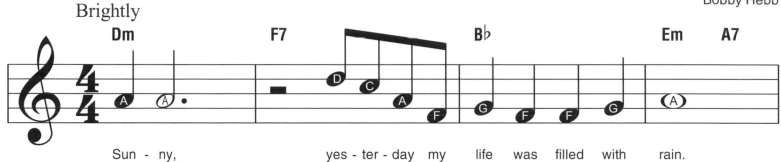

Sun - ny, yes - ter - day my life was filled with rain.

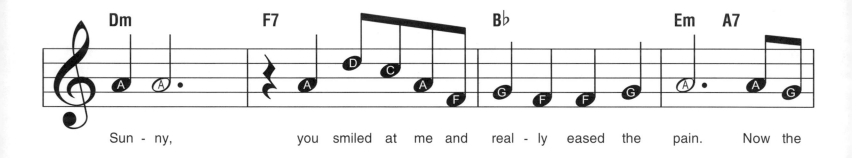

Sun - ny, you smiled at me and real - ly eased the pain. Now the

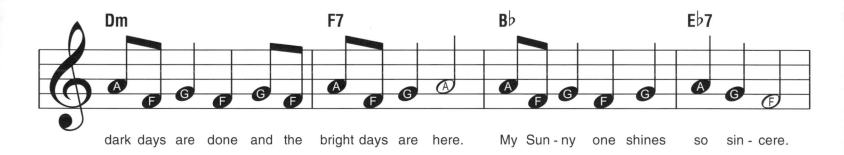

dark days are done and the bright days are here. My Sun - ny one shines so sin - cere.

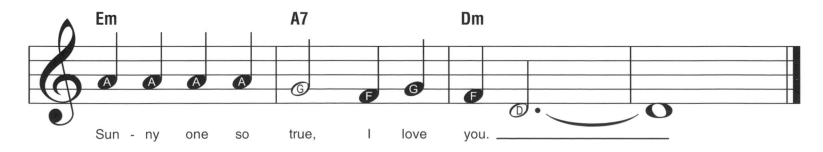

Sun - ny one so true, I love you. _____

You Are So Beautiful

Tears in Heaven

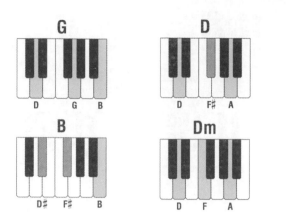
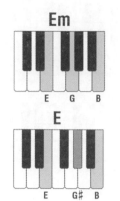
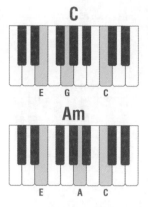

Words and Music by Eric Clapton
and Will Jennings

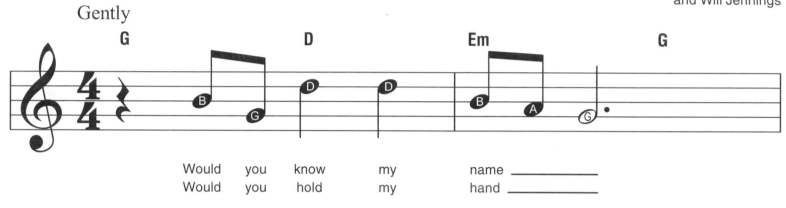

Would you know my name _____
Would you hold my hand _____

if I saw you in heav - en?
if I saw you in heav - en?

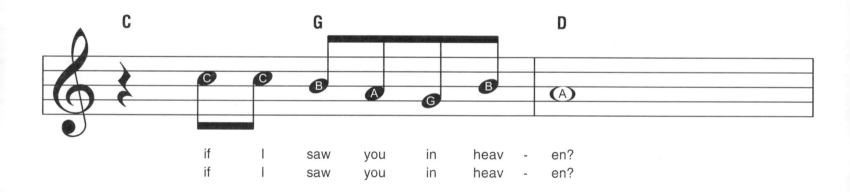

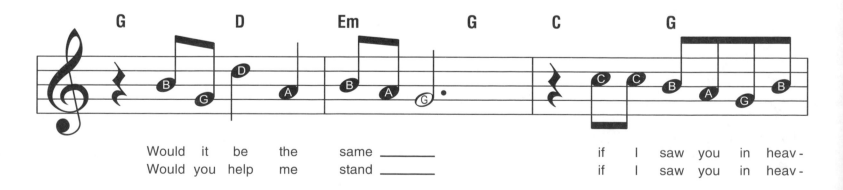

Would it be the same _____
Would you help me stand _____

if I saw you in heav-
if I saw you in heav-

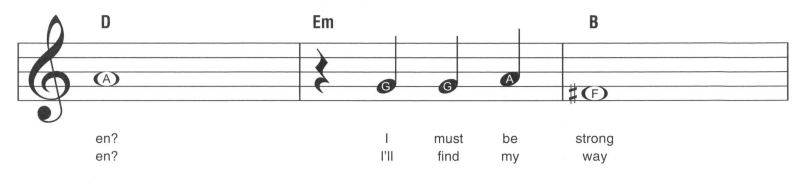

en?   I   must   be   strong
en?   I'll   find   my   way

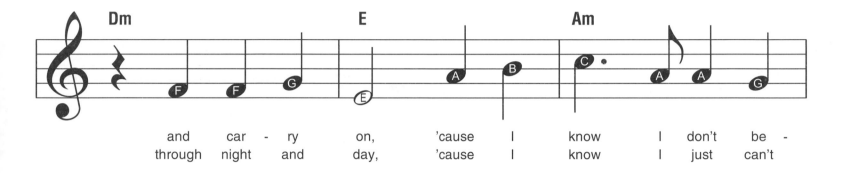

and   car - ry   on,   'cause   I   know   I   don't   be -
through   night   and   day,   'cause   I   know   I   just   can't

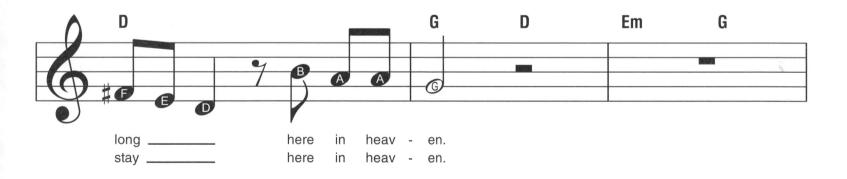

long _____ here   in   heav - en.
stay _____ here   in   heav - en.

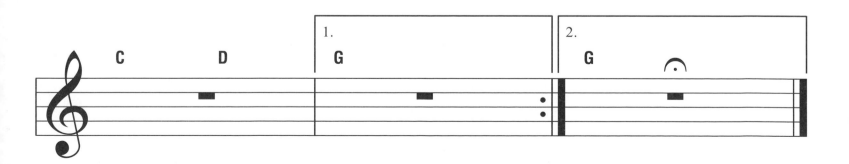

Time After Time

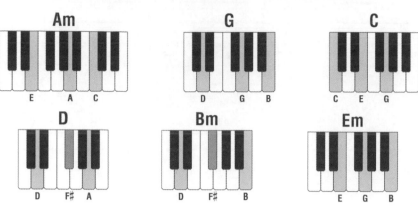

Words and Music by Cyndi Lauper
and Rob Hyman

Moderately

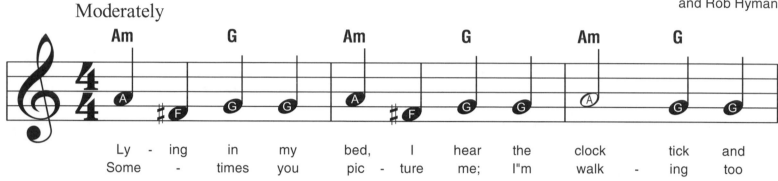

Ly - ing in my bed, I hear the clock tick and
Some - times you pic - ture me; I"m walk - ing too

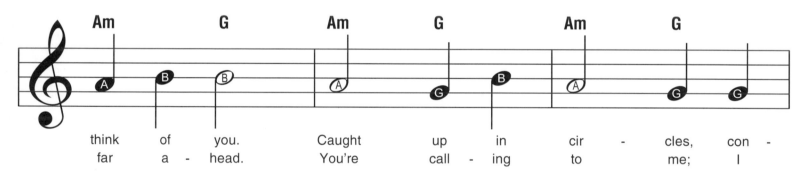

think of you. Caught up in cir - cles, con -
far a - head. You're call - ing to me; I

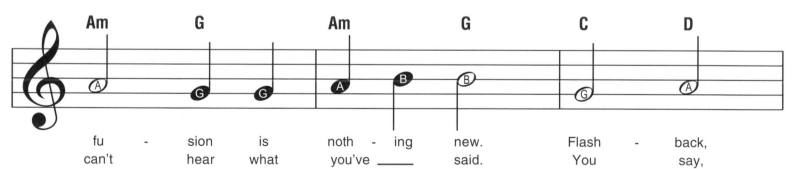

fu - sion is noth - ing new. Flash - back,
can't hear what you've _____ said. You say,

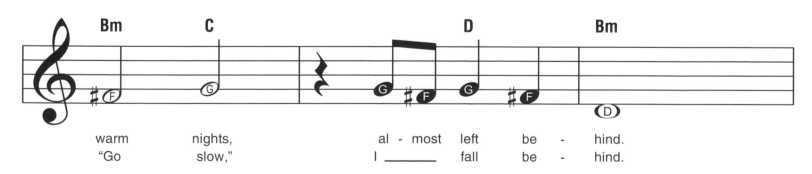

warm nights, al - most left be - hind.
"Go slow," I _____ fall be - hind.

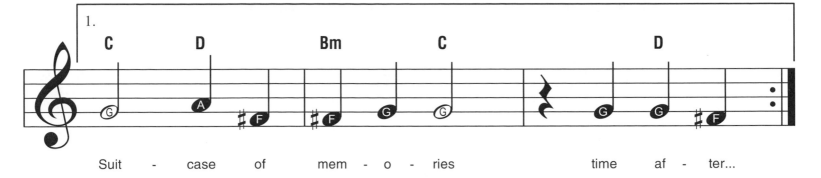

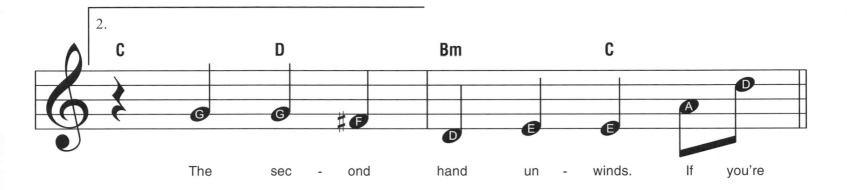

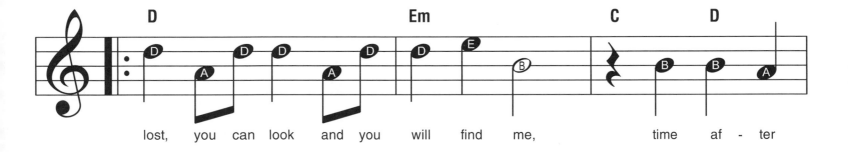

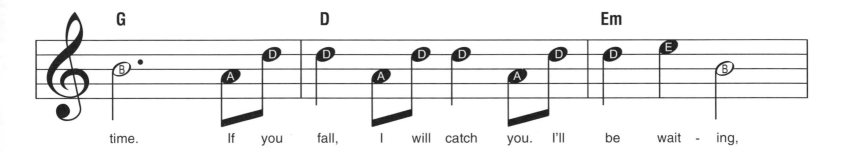

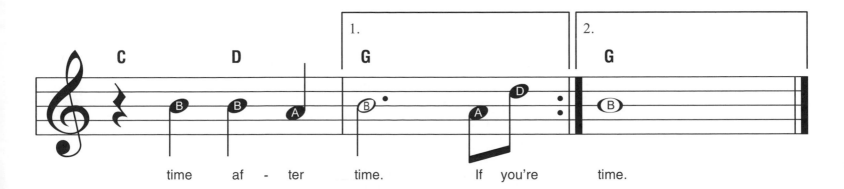

We've Only Just Begun

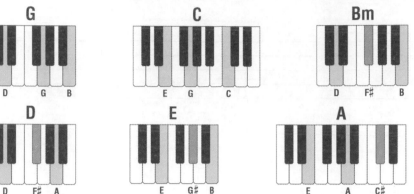
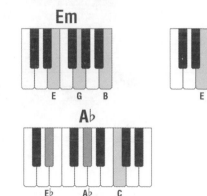
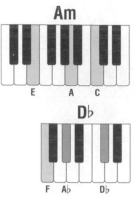

Words and Music by Roger Nichols
and Paul Williams

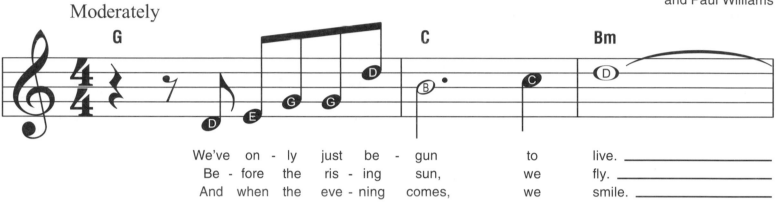

We've on-ly just be-gun to live. _____
Be-fore the ris-ing sun, we fly. _____
And when the eve-ning comes, we smile. _____

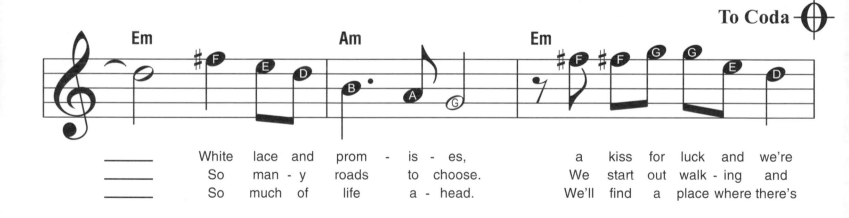

_____ White lace and prom-is-es, a kiss for luck and we're
_____ So man-y roads to choose. We start out walk-ing and
_____ So much of life a-head. We'll find a place where there's

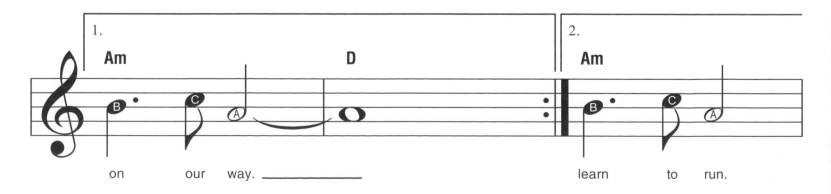

1.
on our way. _____

2.
learn to run.

What the World Needs Now Is Love

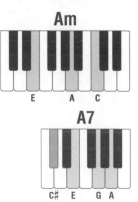
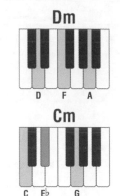
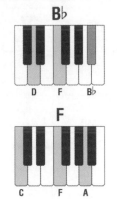
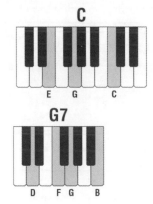

Lyric by Hal David
Music by Burt Bacharach

Moderate Shuffle

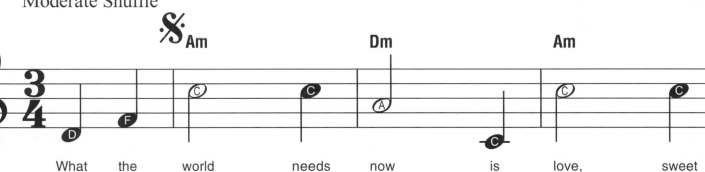

What the world needs now is love, sweet

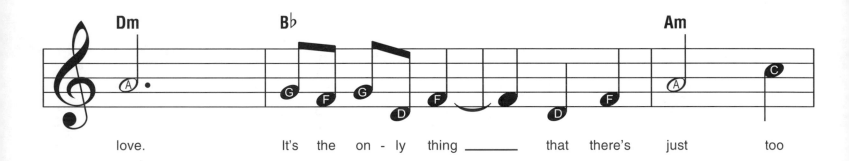

love. It's the on-ly thing _____ that there's just too

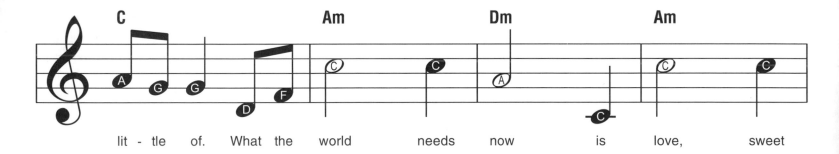

lit-tle of. What the world needs now is love, sweet

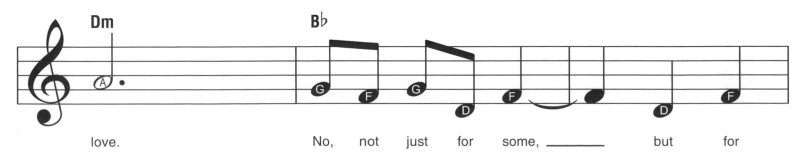

love. No, not just for some, _____ but for

The Wind Beneath My Wings
from the Original Motion Picture BEACHES

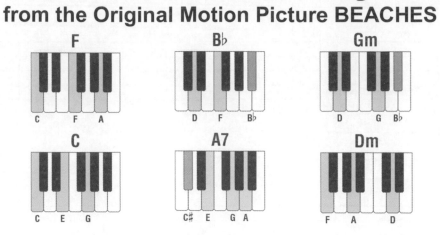

Words and Music by Larry Henley
and Jeff Silbar

It must have been cold there in my shad - ow, _____
So I was the one with all my glo - ry, _____

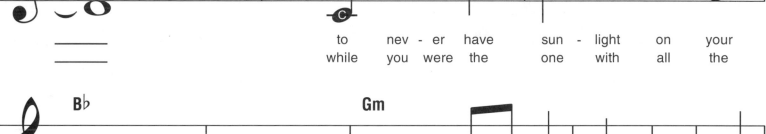

_____ to nev - er have sun - light on your
while you were the one with all your

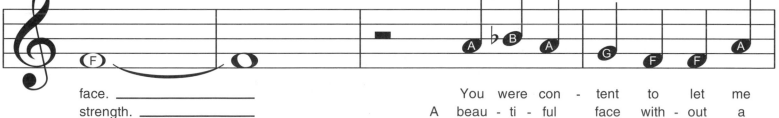

face. _____ You were con - tent to let me
strength. _____ A beau - ti - ful face with - out a

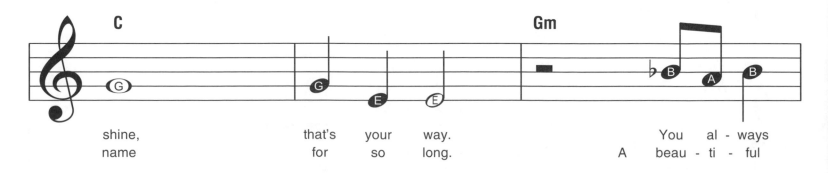

shine, that's your way. You al - ways
name for so long. A beau - ti - ful

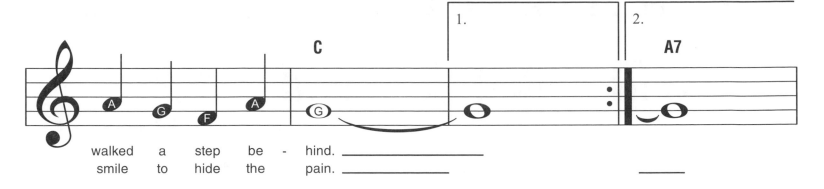

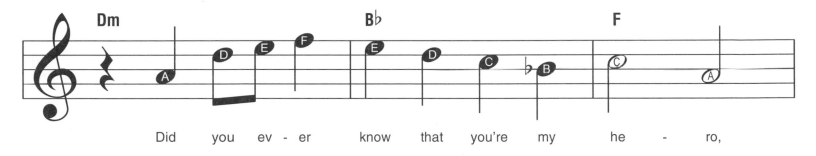

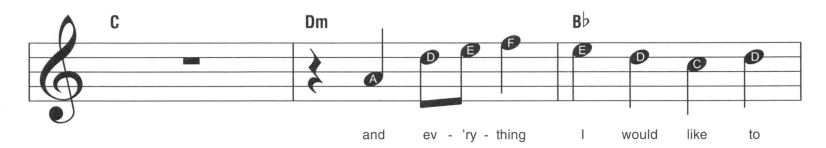

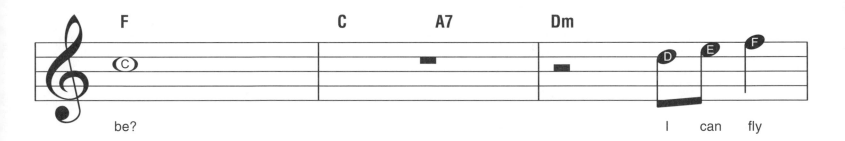

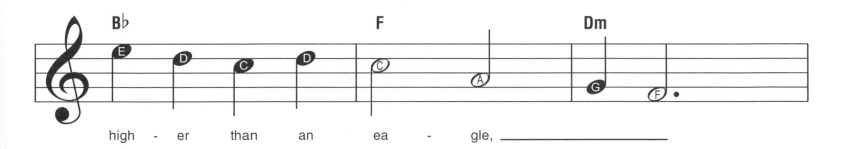

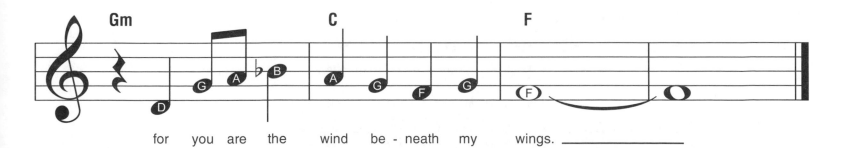

With a Little Help from My Friends

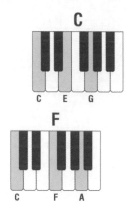 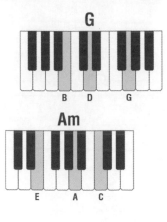 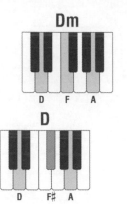 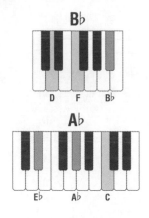

Words and Music by John Lennon
and Paul McCartney

Moderate Shuffle

What would you think if I sang out of tune? Would you
Lend me your ears and I'll sing you a song, Would and I'll

stand up and walk out on me?
try not to sing out of

key. Oh, I get

by with a lit-tle help from my friends. Mm, I get

high with a lit-tle help from my friends. Mm, I'm gon-na

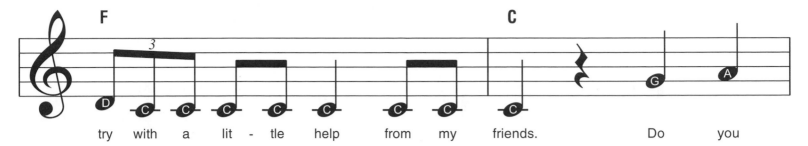

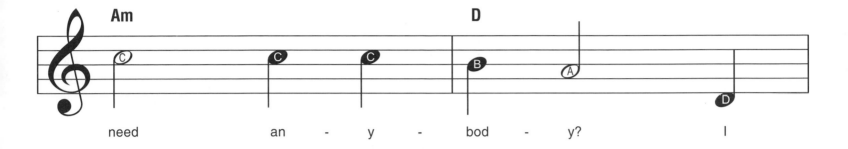

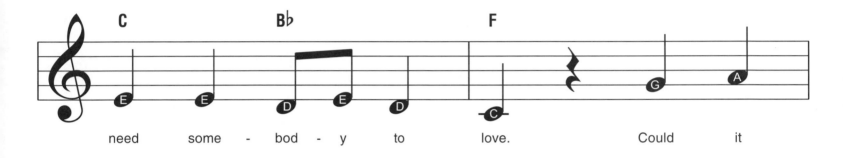

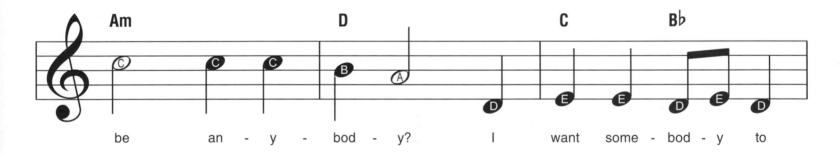

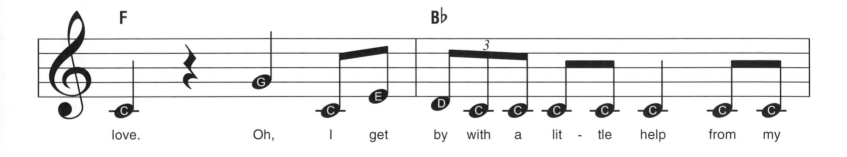

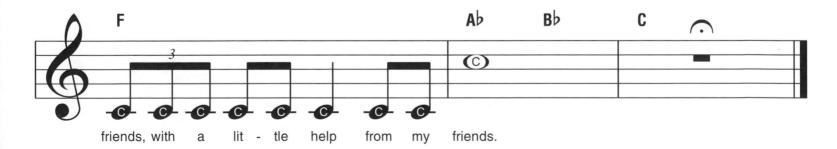

With or Without You

113

You Raise Me Up

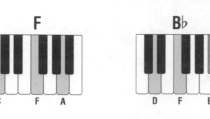
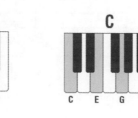
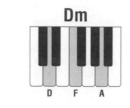

Words and Music by Brendan Graham
and Rolf Lovland

When I am down and, oh, my soul so wea - ry, when trou - bles

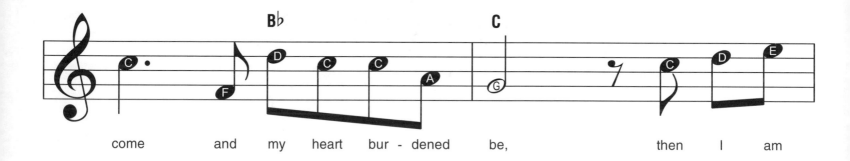

come and my heart bur - dened be, then I am

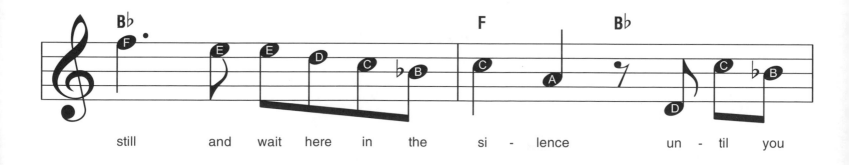

still and wait here in the si - lence un - til you

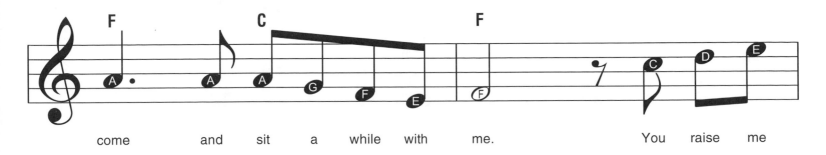

come and sit a while with me. You raise me

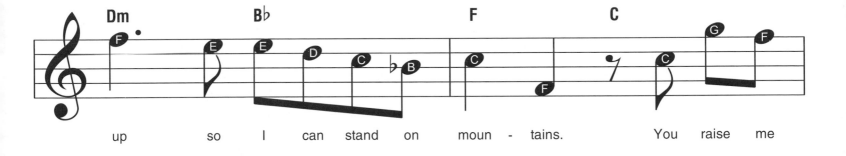

up so I can stand on moun - tains. You raise me

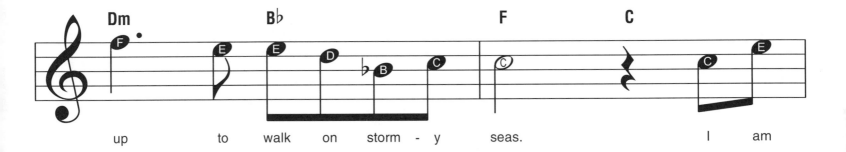

up to walk on storm - y seas. I am

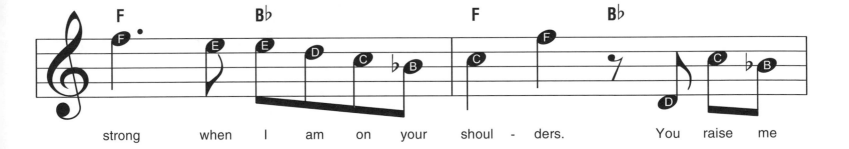

strong when I am on your shoul - ders. You raise me

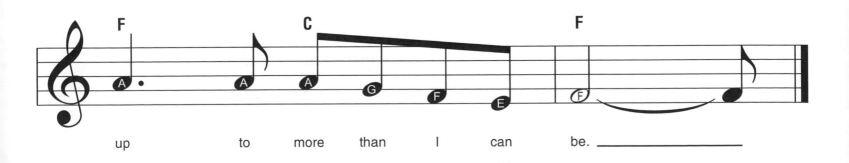

up to more than I can be. _____

You're the Inspiration

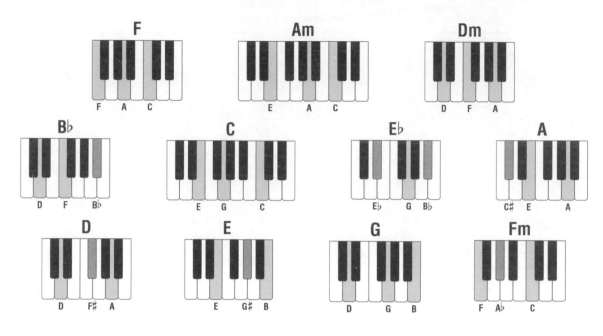

Words and Music by Peter Cetera
and David Foster

Moderately

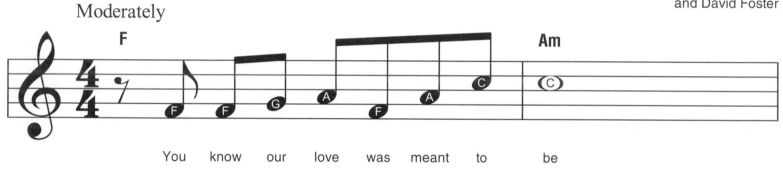

You know our love was meant to be

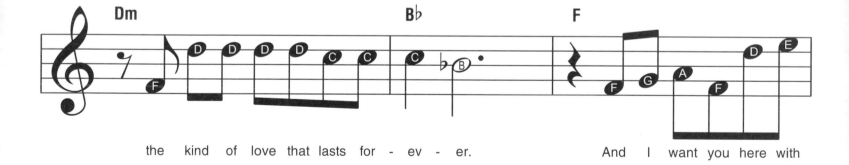

the kind of love that lasts for - ev - er.   And I want you here with

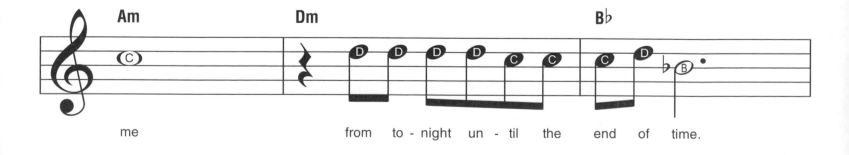

me   from to - night un - til the end of time.

You've Got a Friend

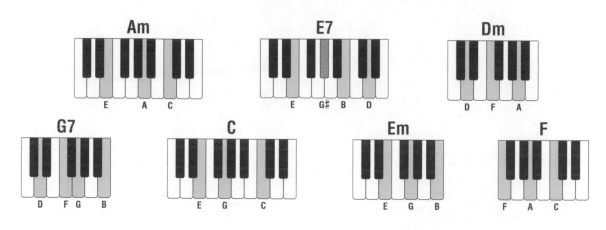

Words and Music by
Carole King

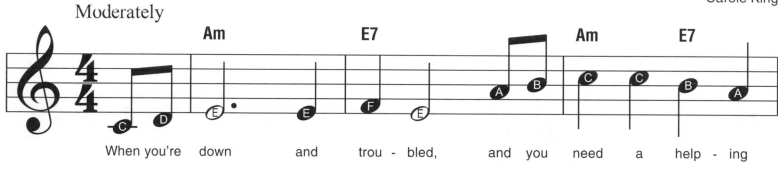

When you're down and trou-bled, and you need a help-ing

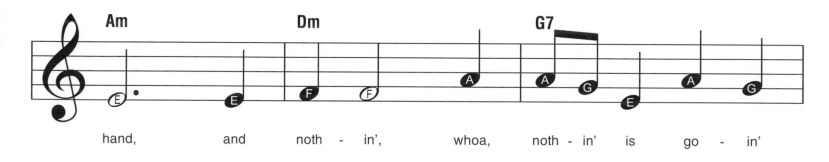

hand, and noth-in', whoa, noth-in' is go-in'

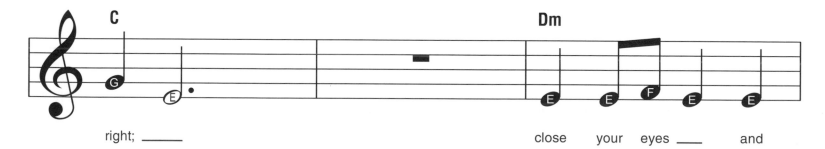

right; _____ close your eyes _____ and

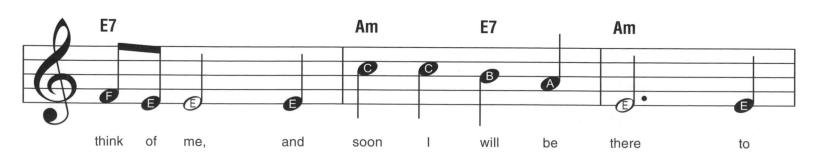

think of me, and soon I will be there to

119

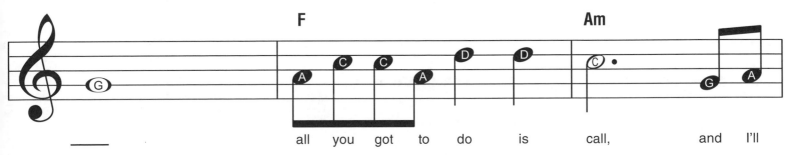